To Julie
with Love

CONTROLLING
OTHERS
FOR LOVE AND PROFIT

If you believe that, then you better wake up.

Controlling others is not the solution …
it is the problem.

Published by
Evolution Impressions
www.evolutionimpressions.com

Foreword by
Lloyd Steven Sieden
www.MysticMandalaImages.com

Illustrations, Cover Design, and Photography by
Peter-Fromme Douglas
www.fromme-douglas.com

Edited by Webmaster
Brandi Jasmine
http://www.brandijasmine.com

Quinn Incorporated
P.O. Box 851
W. Dundee, IL 60118-0851 USA

www.ControllingOthers.com
E-Mail: Quinn@ControllingOthers.com

Printed in the United States of America

First Edition
ISBN: 0-9754417-0-1

QUINN
FOUR E's OF EXCELLENCE

CONTROLLING OTHERS FOR LOVE AND PROFIT

James Roswell Quinn

Evolution impressions
building your image through print

Contents

PART TWO: *Four E's of Excellence*

PART THREE: *Four E's of Excellence* in Action

Dedicated to my wife and children.

I love you "Quinntillions."

Businessman, statesman, inventor, futurist,
architect of the geodesic dome,
and the man who coined the phrase
'Spaceship Earth' …

R. Buckminster Fuller has one of the longest listings
in the history of *Who's Who in America*.

Foreword

Lloyd Steven Sieden, Author

Buckminster Fuller's Universe ... His Life and Times

Now is the time, we are the people. This has been proclaimed by many societies throughout recorded history, but never has it been truer than at this critical moment in the evolution of humankind. We stand at a juncture when, as my mentor Buckminster Fuller wrote on the Valentine's Day prior to his passing on in 1983 ... *"The cosmic question has been asked. Are humans a worthwhile to Universe invention?"*

We find ourselves in the last stages of a great cosmic final examination. We are being tested, and our exam can be boiled down to one simple question we can ask ourselves in each and every one of our actions, *"Am I choosing love or fear?"*

This choice has challenged individuals since the dawn of time, but it has far more meaning at this time when so many have the capacity to destroy so much or to contribute so much with such a small amount of effort. We humans now have the capability to create heaven on Earth or to destroy ourselves and much of our tiny Living Spaceship Earth.

> *"Limits are what we fear."*
>
> ... R. Buckminster Fuller

Bucky Fuller also had the brilliant insight to recognize why this choice of love over fear is actually quite logical today but was not rational for our ancestors even a few decades ago. In the 1930's, Fuller was the first person to do a thorough accounting of all Earth's resources and to determine that we were continually doing "more with less." He then surmised that our "more with lessing" would eventually create a world in which there was enough for everyone, and he sought to determine when that would take place.

His calculations led him to predict that that shift would occur in 1976, and it has now been proven that in 1976 humankind became so efficient that there was and still is enough food to feed everyone on Earth. That statistic also applies to all other resources including non-physical ones such as love.

There is enough of everything, but most of us continue to react from the mindset of pre-1976 when we had to fight for "our share" and to make sure that our family and friends had what they needed. We did this out of fear, and it was valid prior to the 1976 transition. Now, more than ever, we need to recognize that there is enough for everyone and to begin contributing and sharing wholeheartedly. In other words, we need to act out of love rather than out of fear.

The question then becomes, how does one individual contribute his or her best? How can you and I really manifest what is deep within our hearts, make the most difference, and give our individual gifts in the most effective manner possible?

This seems like a difficult challenge until one considers the great women and men who have done just that in spite of a climate in which a World that works for everyone was not practical, because there simply was not enough to go around. Those brave individuals sacrificed much on behalf of others. They gave of themselves in ways we can only describe as heroic even though their peers often perceived them as unstable at best.

Those wise ancestors of ours often used a strategy that each of us can also employ. Bucky Fuller called it being a trimtab. They looked to see where they could make the most difference with the least effort, thereby allowing them to do much more with very little.

> *"A large ship goes by, and then comes the rudder. On the edge of the rudder is a miniature rudder called a trimtab. Moving that trimtab builds a low pressure which turns the rudder that steers the gigantic ship with almost no effort. One individual can be a trimtab, making a major difference."*
>
> … R. Buckminster Fuller

James Roswell Quinn has done just that with much of his life. Rather than devoting the majority of his time to one-on-one consultation, "Ross" shares his talents and insights with groups of people. And with this book, he expands the number of people he can reach markedly.

This same leverage / trimtab principle is available to each and every one of us. We may not be the people who stand in front of a room or write a book, but we have a responsibility to uncover our unique talents and gifts and share them with the World in as potent a manner as possible. Within our World that works for everyone that has emerged since 1976, we are all vital, and once we recognize the truth of our global shift, we become accountable for acting and leading from a position of love in all aspects of our lives.

We need more people who reflect this perspective of love rather than the fear that has dominated our society since the dawn of recorded history. We need "average individuals," as Bucky Fuller and most of our genuinely great leaders called themselves, to step forward into their true calling.

> *"Humanity is taking its final examination.*
> *We have come to an extraordinary moment when*
> *it doesn't have to be you or me anymore.*
> *There is enough for all."*
>
> … R. Buckminster Fuller

Ross has been on the leading edge of supporting this emerging reality and the transformation that it offers to each and every crewmember aboard Spaceship Earth. He has dedicated his life to that challenge, and after years of prodding, he has finally put some of his thoughts onto the written page.

More important to me, he is sharing the wealth of his personal experience obtained over the course of presenting several thousand seminars and workshops as well as consulting with an untold number of individuals. That experience is of primary importance because as Bucky Fuller and so many of our wisest forebears taught - don't believe anything you hear. Trust only your personal experience or the experience of those few individuals you know to be of impeccable integrity.

Whether or not Ross qualifies as someone of impeccable integrity is not the issue. Even though I have known him for many years, I would not ask you to believe a word that he writes or says. I would and have, however, compared his words and ideas to my personal experience. I have utilized many of the techniques he teaches, and, in my personal experience, he has a great deal to offer at this critical juncture in the evolution of humankind.

But don't believe me either. Try what he says, and see how it fits for you. Do as Bucky Fuller and so many who have risen to the highest levels as heartfelt leaders have done. Keep searching and adopt what you find works for you. This will support you in recognizing and embracing humankind's shift from a global culture of fear to one based on love.

This is a journey on which many have embarked. It may not always be smooth sailing, but I can assure you that it is the only way our children and their children will survive and prosper. So, I invite you to join those of us on this path of love where each individual finds and shares her or his true Self.

I invite you to take the path of love to heart and become what Fuller called a trimtab on behalf of all humankind. Each of us can make an enormous difference. We can contribute our gifts to one another and, in the process, receive the rewards of being gifted with the talents of others. On this path the choice of love over fear must be maintained in all areas of our lives.

When making that decision we do not have to sacrifice anything. The path of love is a path of joy. It promotes a sense of wellbeing for all who choose it and all who come into contact with those walking it. It brings forth the best in each of us, and calls us to greater challenges and possibilities. It opens doorways that we did not know existed and allows for the magic called synergy to blossom within our lives and the lives of those we touch.

This is the reality that must soon become the norm. It offers hope and much more. In choosing love as a way to live and lead, each of us helps to lay the foundation for an entirely new civilization in which we manifest the often imagined heaven on Earth. That possibility is here now. It lies within each of us if we only take the time to look. Turn the pages of this book gently, and you will surely find clues to your personal journey on this path.

Lloyd Steven Sieden

Bucky's tombstone reads ... *"Call Me Trimtab"*

"Whether humanity is to continue and comprehensively prosper on Spaceship Earth depends entirely on the integrity of the human individuals and not on the political and economic systems."

… R. Buckminster Fuller

The Four **E**'s of Excellence

ETHICS
X
C
ENTHUSIASM
L
L
EVALUATION
N
C
EMPATHY

Introduction

The Leadership Evolution

Books, keynotes, and workshops on leadership abound. However, while most of these management tools, sales techniques, and relationship strategies are successful in at least some situations and with certain people, the vast majority miss the point:

> All attempts to influence or control others are focused on the wrong person.
>
> **Leadership Excellence is the Art of Self-Control**

While everyone may agree that self-control is the answer, the problem is how each person defines it. For some people self-control means toughness: *"I don't get mad, I get even."* For others, it is all about leaving doors open in case something goes wrong: *"I don't have to take this, I'm out of here."* For many, self-control is defined as the ability to refrain from hurting people, even when hurt or angry themselves: *"If you can't say something nice, don't say anything at all."* For yet another group, it means to do whatever it takes to keep from upsetting others: *"If you're happy, I'm happy."*

Statements such as these may be synonymous with 'self-control' to many people; however they are all in actuality a type of control of others. They are either about getting someone **to do** something (such as keeping their commitments or treating you kindly), or to **prevent** them from doing something (such as getting upset or hurting someone else). Unfortunately, whether striving to be helpful or self-serving, the only way to ensure success with these tactics is to establish some kind of *'Position-Power'* over others.

Personal, professional, or global *Position-Power* always flows from the top down. As such, employers, managers, salespeople, elected officials, police officers, parents, spouses, and partners ultimately strive to deal with stress by establishing or enforcing the power of their position, in order to get what they desire.

Position-Power may be blatant, often backed up with orders, threats, demands, hysterics, and ultimatums. However, this manipulation can also be demonstrated in more subtle ways, such as by shutting down, looking sad, backing away, and deception.

While we may claim to be acting for altruistic motivations, at its base, *Position-Power* is the rationalized control of others due to fear. This can be a fear OF others: *"You might hurt me."* However, it can also be a fear FOR others: *"You might hurt yourself."* The bottom line is, whether striving to protect yourself or someone else, leadership by *Position-Power* is nothing more than a *Fear-Based* knee jerk reaction designed to control others.

Position-Based Leaders are ***Fear-Based Reactors.***

The terms are synonymous and interchangeable,
and both are becoming obsolete.

Regardless of the methodology or intent, *Position-Based* leaders are facing increasing resistance. Modern persons in democratic societies do not function under a strict and inflexible hierarchy as our ancestors once did. We resent those who control us, or attempt to control us, even when we are told it is for *"our own good."* The reverse is also true. Others resent us when we control them, or attempt to control them, even when we tell them it is for *"their own good"* ... just ask any teenager.

Controlled children may not rebel but, at best, they will have a limited relationship with their parents when they become adults. A spouse can control their partner or children but, in so doing, will destroy their love, respect, and affection. Dishonest or incongruent salespeople may initially make money, but it is rare when sales from repeat business and referrals occur. Dictatorships may seem to be effective, but history teaches us that assassinations and revolutions are the inevitable outcome.

In the short term, the creation of a *Fear-Based* environment can give a business the illusion of effectiveness. However, employees with high levels of self-worth will find a better place to work. Those who remain usually see the levels of fear increase, in direct proportion to decreased corporate results. The cycle will continue until excellence and passion are stifled. In a world where innovation and creativity are needed for long-term business success, companies operating within this paradigm cannot flourish.

Traditional leadership methodologies are all effective to some degree.

However, when motives are *Fear-Based,* these systems become *Position-Power* control tools. While they may appear successful, results are usually temporary, and there is always a price to pay. Resentment and resistance ultimately lead to sabotage, diminished results, and even destruction. The good news is, there is an alternative to *Position-Based* leadership. The old *Fear-Based* patterns are changing.

Today, there is a shift away from *Position-Based* leadership. People are beginning to realize they are merely creating new problems whenever they justify *Fear-Based* reactions to challenging circumstances. *Position-Based* leadership is losing ground to effective, innovative, and forward thinking leaders. Whether the desire is for loving relationships, joyful families, business success, or effective government, it is becoming increasingly apparent that positive results will come <u>through</u> leaders, not <u>from</u> them.

To be effective, a leader must become aware of his or her *Fear-Based* reactions, and make necessary decisions to overcome them. Leadership Excellence is a skill that can be sharpened and made more effective by increasing the capacity to think, reason, and make conscious choices. The *Four E's of Excellence* teaches you how to overcome stress and create positive results, first by becoming aware of your own negative *Fear-Based* reactions and then by being responsible for changing <u>your</u> behavior.

> The reactions of anyone, other than yourself, are merely measures of your own effectiveness … or lack thereof.

The *"Four E's of Excellence"* are Ethics, Enthusiasm, Evaluation, and Empathy. Present in all truly effective leaders, these elements could also be defined as Vision, Joy, Determination, and Compassion. Regardless of the names we assign to these qualities, self-control is needed to demonstrate them all, especially in the face of negative circumstances.

This book is not a philosophical attempt to define an unattainable Utopian ideal of leadership. It is a description of an evolving phenomenon. It is a "tool-box" of practical techniques for breaking non-productive patterns, achieving goals, reducing stress, developing trust, and creating consensus.

The concepts and techniques in the *Four E's of Excellence* are more than theory. They have been refined over the last 30 years, in more than 2,500 personal and professional development seminars in the United States, New

Zealand, Canada, and Israel. They have helped tens of thousands of people overcome everything from minor irritations to unimaginable tragedies. Many of their stories are included in order to assist you in using the *Four E's of Excellence*, 'For Ease of Excellence' in solving your personal and professional challenges.

These are difficult times. Intimate relationships often seem to cause more frustration than fulfillment. Many families are in turmoil. A large number of corporations are floundering or failing. A new international crisis seems to arise daily. Most people are finding themselves fighting threats on several different fronts. We have enough victims, we need leaders.

We are in the midst of a leadership evolution.

Leadership Based on *Position-Power* is History.

The evolution in leadership will influence our intimate, family, business, community, national, and global affairs. I challenge you to use the ideas and concepts in this book, especially Chapter 10, to create personal and professional results not just <u>in</u> your life, but also <u>with</u> your life.

Stop fighting against what you do not want, and fight to create what you do want. There is a difference.

Welcome to the quest,

James Roswell Quinn

PART ONE

Fear-Based Reactions

Fear-Based Reactions:

Automatic negative behaviors
in the face of real or perceived threats.

Chapter 1

The Four *Fear-Based* Reactions

We are all looking for happier and more fulfilled lives. Whether our desires are modest or spectacular, we often go to extreme lengths to get what we want. While we are all hoping to get lucky, we inherently know one thing; it is our own actions which have the primary impact on our success or failure.

Yet somehow, time after time, we self-sabotage. Sometimes we are blind to what we are doing, and of course, nothing changes. At other times, however, we are fully aware that we are acting in a counter-productive or destructive manner … but just cannot stop ourselves. It is our habitual negative behaviors which can make us each our own worst enemy.

Any such pattern, whether conscious or unconscious, is based upon fear. It could be a fear of getting something we do not want (such as rejection or physical pain), or a fear of losing something we do want (such as a relationship or a job). Either way …

> Our *Fear-Based* reactions are the true barriers to personal growth and professional development.

If you took Psychology 101, you probably remember the 'Fight or Flight' survival theory. Basically, this concept describes the two *Fear-Based* reactions of our ancient ancestors. When faced with physical threats, they would either attack or retreat.

However, these were not the only two *Fear-Based* reactions. There is a third form known as the "Freeze." When unable to attack a threat or run away, early people also learned to protect themselves by 'playing dead' or 'hiding in a cave' hoping the threat would go away.

While we may think of ourselves as modern, rational beings, we still tend to react to threats much as people did ages ago … even though our methods are usually a little more subtle. For example, couples argue and workers rant (Fight). Personal relationships break-up or divorce, and people quit business relationships (Flight). Spouses shut each other out and employees immerse themselves into computers or busy-work (Freeze).

We are each confronted with examples of Fight, Flight, and Freeze on a daily basis … but there is yet another *Fear-Based* reaction which does not fit these three older categories. The fourth reactive category is the 'Facade' … a false front, a lie. Whether used as an attempt to hurt someone through deception or to protect another with a 'white-lie,' a Facade reaction is a camouflage of the truth.

In the modern world, the four *Fear-Based* reactions do not require the pre-requisite of actual danger. Simply feeling threatened is enough to trigger them. Reality and perceptions have become equal under the reaction process.

When reacting from fear, the brain believes whatever you tell it.

The brain does not know the difference between what is real … and what it perceives to be real.

All *Fear-Based* reactions can be appropriate responses to threatening circumstances. Modern problems stem from the fact they can also become habits, which may evolve into destructive patterns, with considerable personal and professional consequences.

Instead of leaving your life to chance, the key to success is to identify and overcome your *Fear-Based* reactions to challenging people and negative circumstances. Think of this book as your 'tool kit' in this quest.

Begin by knowing that all of us demonstrate each of the four *Fear-Based* reactions in different situations. However each of us has also elevated one or two of them to a 'preferred' status. By becoming aware of your more obvious *Fear-Based* reactions, it will then become easier for you to identify your subtle ones. As you read the following descriptions, determine your more common patterns.

The Four *Fear-Based* Reactions

FIGHT FLIGHT

FREEZE FACADE

The "FIGHT" Reaction

When demonstrating Fight reactions, you give ultimatums, become sarcastic, or attack. Whether you are actively seeking to fix something, finish something, or to punish someone, you say exactly what you mean. You are, or appear to be, unconcerned about the needs and feelings of others.

You will hear yourself asking **"What"** types of questions …
*"**What's** your problem?" … "**What** are you going to do about it?"*

When You Are Consumed With RESULTS,
Your Primary Characteristic Tends to Be JUDGMENTAL.

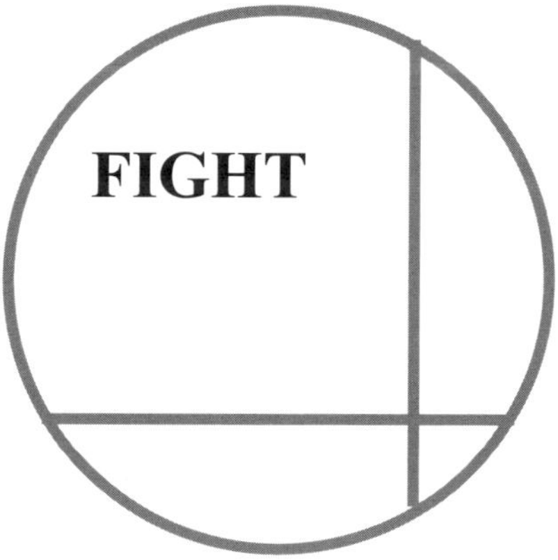

"I don't get mad, I get even."
"If you want something done right, you've got to do it yourself."
"The end justifies the means,"

Other Characteristics:

Aggressive	Manipulative	Arrogant	Sarcastic	Critical
Demanding	Intimidating	Insensitive	Offensive	Argumentative

The extreme Fight reaction is to become PARANOID

The "FLIGHT" Reaction

When demonstrating Flight reactions, you panic, make excuses, rush, "motor-mouth," or interrupt others. Whether you are trying to find something for someone, make it to an appointment, or get away from someone, you say the first thing that comes to your mind. You are not listening to anyone else.

You will hear yourself asking **"Who or When"** types of questions …
*"**Who** do you think you are?" … "**When** is my appointment?"*

When You Are Consumed With a RELATIONSHIP(S),
Your Primary Characteristic Tends to Be FRANTIC.

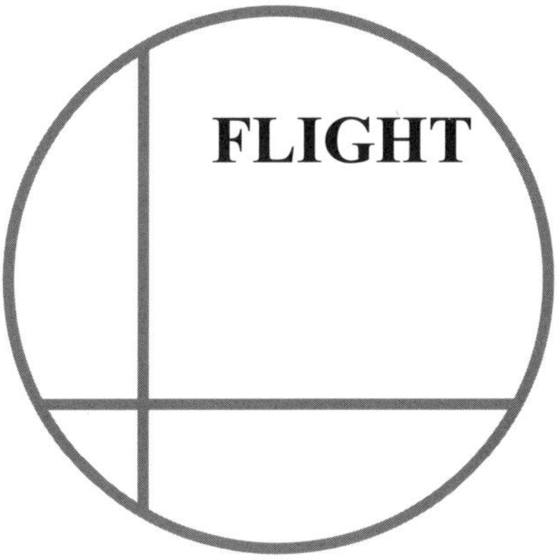

"I don't have to take this, I'm out of here."
"Don't worry about it … I'll take care of it later."
"I've got too much to do and not enough time to do it."

Other Characteristics:

Distracted	Overwhelming	Harried	Panicked	Hyperactive
Impulsive	Hurried	Excitable	Pushy	Scattered

The extreme Flight reaction is to become HISTRIONIC

The "FREEZE" Reaction

When demonstrating Freeze reactions, you become analyzing, isolated, and generally avoid others. Whether you are trying to get something right, figure something out, or are avoiding a relationship, you do not even speak until you have had the time to collect your thoughts.

You will hear yourself internally asking **"How"** types of questions....
*"**How** can you say that to me?" ... "**How** can I do all of this?"*

When You Are Consumed With TASKS,
Your Primary Characteristic Tends to Be OVERWHELMED.

"I don't want to talk about it."
"In the time it takes to explain, I can do it myself."
"If you can't say something nice, don't say anything at all."

Other Characteristics:

Anxious	Inward	Picky	Withdrawn	Apprehensive
Serious	Shameful	Tense	Isolated	Shut-Down

The extreme Freeze reaction is to become AVOIDANT

The "FACADE" Reaction

When demonstrating Facade reactions, you strive to make things look better than they really are. Whether you are trying to protect yourself or someone else, you say only what you think others can handle … or what you feel they want to hear.

You will ask yourself or others **"Why"** types of questions …
*"**Why** me?" … "**Why** can't we just get along?"*
*"Nothing's wrong, **why** do you ask?"*

When You Are Consumed With FEELINGS and EMOTIONS,
Your Primary Characteristic Tends to Be WORRIED.

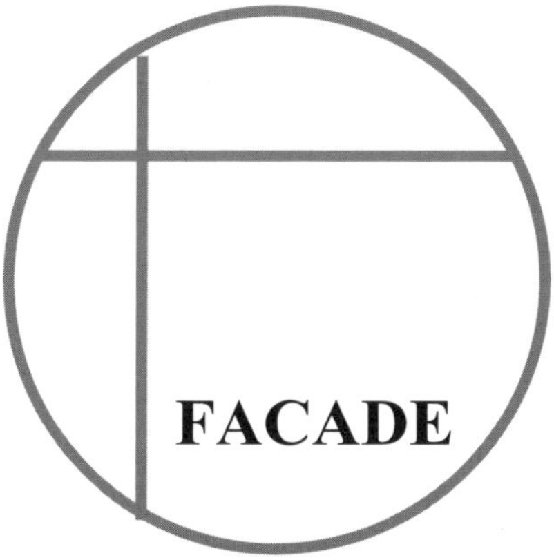

I say one thing to your face, but I'm thinking something else.
Out loud, *"I'm fine. I'm just fine."* Inside, *"I'm hurt and angry."*
Out loud, *"I'll buy your product."* Inside, *"I'll cancel tomorrow."*

Other Characteristics:

Intimidated	Defensive	Phony	Subordinate	Guarded
Guilty	Insecure	Inferior	Fragile	Needy

The extreme Facade reaction is to become DEPENDENT

EXTREME *Fear-Based* Reactions

As people develop habitual reactive patterns, over time they risk losing self-control and demonstrating EXTREME *Fear-Based* reactions, which resemble psychological 'disorders.' These disorders are Paranoid, Histrionic, Avoidant, and Dependent (Abnormal Psychology, Rosenban & Seligman, 1989). To understand the need for self-control in times of stress, observe the results when people totally lose self-control …

1) The effects on a person having EXTREME *Fear-Based* Reactions.

2) The effects EXTREME *Fear-Based* Reactions have on others.

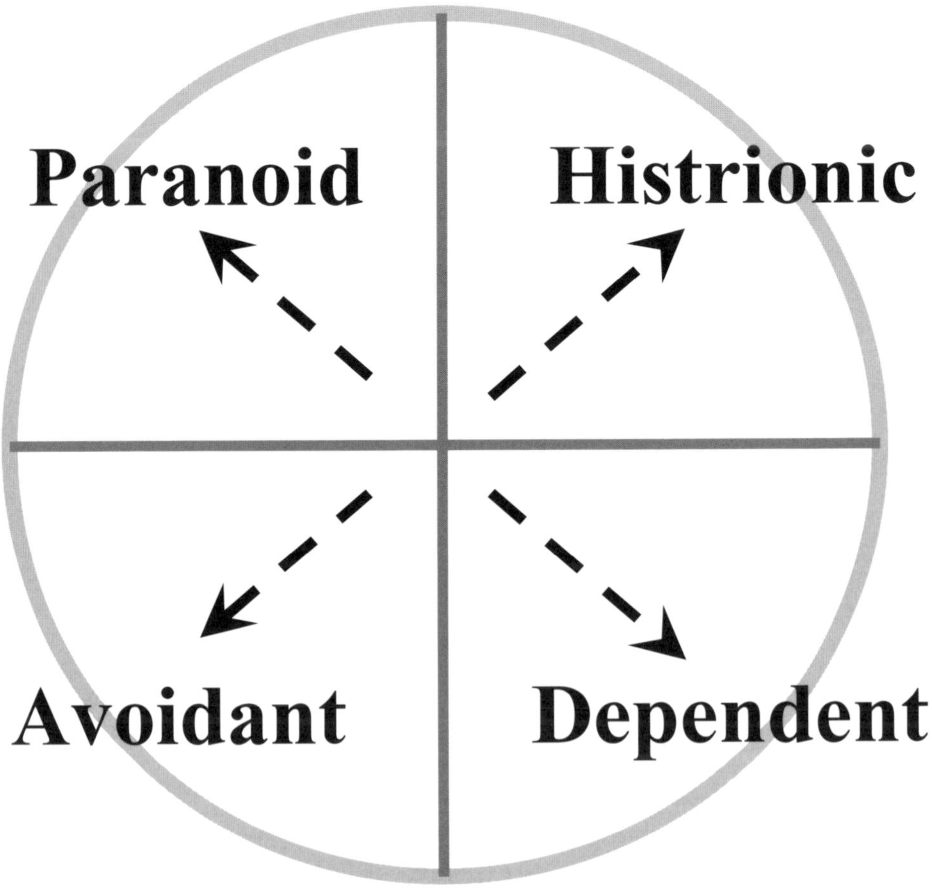

The Fight Reaction can become Paranoid behavior:

When the Fight reaction becomes a habit, we not only attack real threats, we eventually begin to attack perceived threats as well. As we become more sensitive to perceived threats, more circumstances trigger this reaction, and paranoia eventually sets in. Woody Allen once said, *"It isn't paranoia if they really ARE out to get you."* However, if you have ever spent any time with a paranoid person, you know how any little thing can make them lose control.

The Flight Reaction can become Histrionic behavior:

When we were kids, my grandmother used to tell us, *"Quit running around like chickens with your heads cut off."* Some people leave jobs or relationships at the first sign of a challenge. Others become chatterboxes and push others away with fidgety, hyperactive behavior. Either way, the results are the same. People who run away from problems are usually running toward new ones. The only thing that changes is how much easier it becomes to trigger the next histrionic episode.

The Freeze Reaction can become Avoidant behavior:

The Freeze reaction can easily grow into a pattern of avoidance, mostly because of the temporary sense of peace it can bring. However, the long-term costs of shutting down overshadow any short-term gains. Corporations need leaders who are quickly able to address challenging situations, and predict problems rather than avoiding them. All relationships require active involvement. Spouses, partners, and parents, who put on blinders to small problems, only guarantee larger problems later.

The Facade Reaction can become Dependent behavior:

When a person spends considerable time worrying about the feelings and reactions of others, Facade reactions can develop into outright lies. These often take the form of "little" white lies, but they are lies nonetheless. Increasingly, as this behavior becomes one of dependence, self-worth slips away. The only way this person can feel good is when someone else makes them feel good. Unfortunately, when another person is in charge of your happiness, they are also in charge of your unhappiness. That person gains control of everything.

SECONDARY *Fear-Based* Reactions

Everyone periodically reacts in each of the four basic ways (Fight, Flight, Freeze, and Facade). Occasionally, even normal people can react in the extreme (Paranoid, Histrionic, Avoidant, and Dependent).

> While we tend to use one *Fear-Based* reaction more often than the rest, most people have a *Secondary* reaction that occurs almost as often.

While a *Secondary* reaction can occur simultaneously with the primary *Fear-Based* reaction, it usually follows immediately afterward. There is a *Primary/Secondary* pattern, which is responsible for a great deal of pain and suffering. Some people verbally or physically abuse their spouse or lover in a fit of rage, then later apologize and promise, *"It will never happen again."* However, the abuse and the promise are eventually repeated. This abuse cycle is the Fight reaction followed by the Facade as a *Secondary* reaction.

My own typical pattern is generally the opposite. Facade is my primary *Fear-Based* reaction. When threatened, I worry about the other person's feelings more than my own. My behavior is affected accordingly, as I do not want to upset anyone. However, if I am feeling attacked or unappreciated, I can move directly into Fight (generally in the form of anger or sarcasm) as my *Secondary* reaction.

Another common scenario is the Facade reaction followed by Flight. People will tell you *"Everything is fine,"* when it is not. Then they run away as quickly as possible: *"I have got to get out of here."* This is the pattern used when a customer places an order one day, but calls to cancel the next.

Many people can have difficulty identifying their primary *Fear-Based* reaction when their *Secondary* reaction occurs frequently, and vice-versa. Do not worry if you have trouble distinguishing them. The important thing is to identify the reaction you are making, *while* you are making it. Then, and only then, you can make a conscious decision to overcome it.

SECONDARY *Fear-Based* Reactions

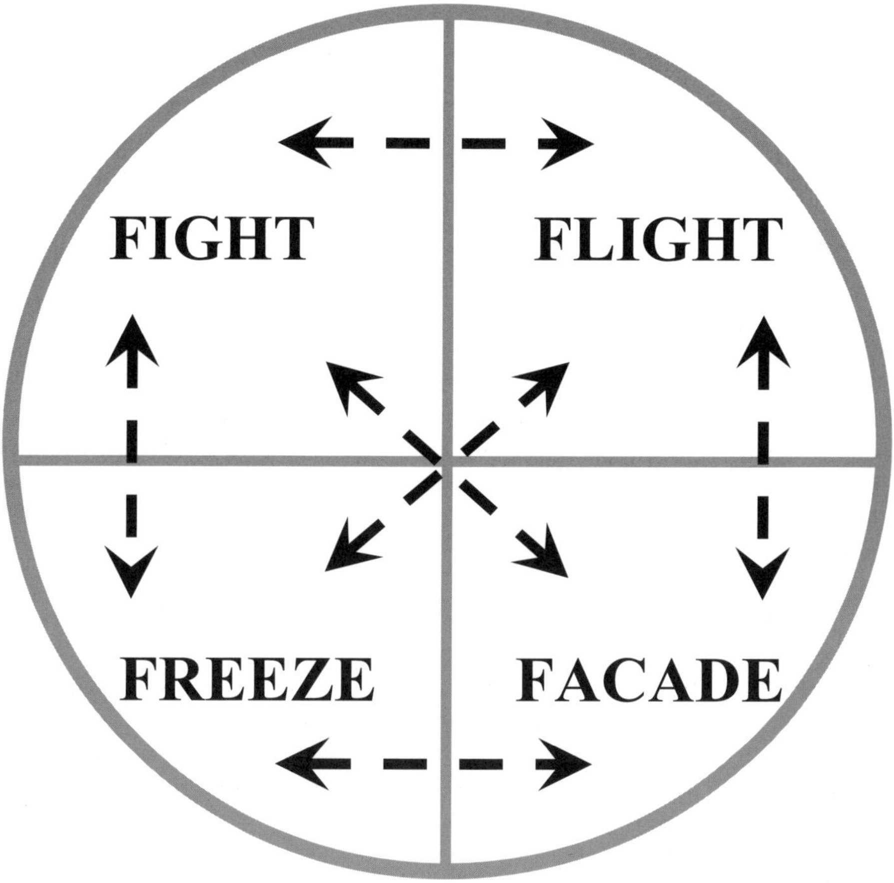

Pre-Actions and *Survival Programs*

People tend to have a *Fear-Based* reaction when first threatened with a new negative situation. If there is any perceived benefit associated with that *Fear-Based* reaction, the behavior is likely to be repeated when faced with the same or similar circumstance.

If this *Fear-Based* reaction it is repeated enough, it eventually occurs prior to the negative circumstance, *"Just in case."* This *Fear-Based* behavior is no longer a reaction ... it is now a *'Pre-Action.'*

> ## *Pre-Actions*
>
> Conscious *Fear-Based* behaviors which occur BEFORE real or perceived negative circumstances, not as a result of them.

For example, a small boy cries when he falls and hurts himself. This is a natural response to pain. However, in our culture he often learns the lesson that it is unacceptable for boys to show their feelings. He may hear something such as, *"Don't be such a baby,"* or the classic, *"If you don't stop crying, I'll give you something to cry about."* He might even get spanked. His father may be cruel and insensitive, or he could simply be concerned his son might get picked on for being a crybaby.

After a while, the child starts to figure it out. One day he hurts himself and starts to cry, but is able to *Pre-Act* and hold back his tears. His father may ignore this victory, or acknowledge it. To the little boy, either response is far superior to being spanked, threatened, or ridiculed.

This is an over-simplified description, and not intended to describe the only possible alternative. Indeed, there are those children for whom a spanking has become the desired circumstance. To them, negative attention is better than no attention at all.

For this little boy, however, the choice to refrain from crying around his father effectively prevents another negative circumstance. You could say it takes wisdom to change a behavior that is creating problems.

The real danger with *Pre-Actions* occurs when they cease being conscious choices, and begin being unconscious behaviors. These *'Survival Programs'* require no thought at all, but often cause bigger problems than they originally prevented.

> People may be ignorant, but they are not stupid.
> There is always some value to a *Fear-Based* reaction.
> Otherwise, this type of behavior would never be demonstrated enough to become a conscious *Pre-Action* ...
>
> and, ultimately, an unconscious *Survival Program.*

Survival Programs themselves are not the problem. They only become the problem when changing circumstances render them ineffective, counter-productive, or even destructive.

The Sand Wasp

Once upon a time, some scientists were studying sand wasps. While observing their eating habits, they discovered a strange habit indigenous to the species.

Every morning the sand wasps scoured the desert for food. Usually they found a dead fly or some other bug. However, instead of eating the meal out in the open, the sand wasps would carry the food back to their respective holes in the sand. For some reason, they would drop their breakfast outside before entering their home. After a few moments, each would return for their food and go back inside to eat.

No sand wasp ever deviated from this behavior. Apparently, over the centuries, natural selection favored sand wasps with two *Survival-Programs*: 1) Never eat outside, and 2) always check for intruders before bringing food inside to eat.

The scientists decided to find out just how firmly this program was ingrained. They observed a sand wasp with a dead horsefly. When it left its food next to the entrance of its hole to check inside, the scientists moved the horsefly a couple of feet away.

The sand wasp returned to get its breakfast and, of course, found nothing. It began to look for food, just as if it never had it in the first place. After a few minutes, the sand wasp found the same horsefly and proceeded to drag it back to its hole, leave it, and again go inside to look for intruders.

Again, the scientists moved the horsefly while the sand wasp was gone. When it returned to find its food missing, the sand wasp began to search for food again … again … and again.

The scientists kept repeating this experiment, always with the same results. The sand wasp finally died of exhaustion and starvation, literally with food in its mouth. The scientists surmised the sand wasp was incapable of changing its *Survival-Program*, even when its behavior was no longer of value … even though the program was killing it.

Moral

A great many sand wasps are disguised as people …
doing the same thing over and over again,
even if it is killing them.

Non-Survival Programs

While *Survival Programs* always have some value, they are often only valuable in the specific situations for which they were created. Since they are unconscious, *Survival Programs* can lose effectiveness and even become invitations to disaster when circumstances change. In this event, they are subject to becoming *Non-Survival Programs,* as with the Sand Wasp.

In the earlier example, the little boy develops a *Survival Program* of withholding his negative feelings. This behavior clearly protects him and placates his father. Everybody gains something. Eventually, the little boy grows up, gets a job, and gets married … but retains his, now unconscious, *Survival Program.*

This *Fear-Based* behavior now creates a strain on both his career and marriage. He has difficulty sharing new ideas at work, and cannot open up with his wife at all. This man does not succeed to his potential in the workplace, because he is afraid to risk the rejection of his ideas.

Additionally, after a few years, his frustrated spouse divorces him because he is emotionally unavailable to her. The behavior, which once served the child, has ceased to serve the adult. It has become a *Non-Survival Program.*

> A valuable *Survival Program* in one environment
> often becomes a destructive *'Non-Survival' Program* in another.

"Look both ways before you cross the street" is a very common admonition by parents who are trying to create safe behavior in their children. Typically, this warning occurs so often that it becomes an automatic *Survival Program*, needing no thought whatsoever. Eventually, it occurs even when the act is unnecessary … like when crossing a one-way street. At this point it has become similar to the Sand Wasp's habit of always checking its hole for intruders, even after a recent investigation has rendered this activity unnecessary.

In this event, the act of looking both ways before crossing the street has the potential of becoming a *Non-Survival Program* capable of causing death and injury. Yes, every year there are those who are struck by cars <u>because</u> they look both ways before crossing a street. I was almost one of them. How can this be?

On my first trip to New Zealand, I was almost run over as I crossed the street. As is my *Survival Program,* I automatically looked to the left to check the road in the direction traffic "normally" comes from. Unfortunately, in New Zealand the traffic travels in the opposite direction.

Traffic was clear to the left so, as usual, I stepped off the curb an instant before I looked to the right … where the traffic was actually coming from. Oops. Fortunately, a wonderfully alert friend pulled me back just before I was flattened by a bus. My *Survival Program* became a *Non-Survival* program because it had me look the <u>wrong way first</u>.

Three Classic *Fear-Based* Programs

1) "Don't talk to strangers," is a classic *Survival Program* which can protect children from harm. However, it frequently shifts from a *Survival* to a *Non-Survival Program* later in life. When your boss tells you to go and find new clients he or she might as well have said, *"Go talk to strangers."*

2) "Eat everything on your plate," is another common *Survival Program.* Following this instruction eliminates ridicule and punishment at the dinner table. However, it goes from a *Survival Program* to a *Non-Survival Program* years later when you have a weight problem … and are not able to leave the table if food is remaining on your plate, even when you have had enough to eat.

3) "Children should be seen and not heard" and ***"Don't speak unless spoken to,"*** are *Survival Programs* that can keep children from being punished in social situations. They become *Non-Survival Programs* when low self-worth and anxiety prevent successful personal and professional relationships.

> Once a *Survival Program* becomes a *Non-Survival Program,*
> it will continue to be self-destructive until you change your behavior
> … but most of us make excuses instead.

"I'm sorry. I haven't slept in two days."

"Of course I'm mad. You broke your promise to me."

"It wasn't my fault. He cut me off."

"I'm overwhelmed. I don't mean to be taking it out on you."

"If you had a childhood like mine, you'd be screwed-up too."

and my personal favorite of all excuses …

"I'm only human."

One of the great "lies" is that mistakes are just learning experiences. Nonsense; mistakes are not learning experiences … unless you actually learn something from them. By continuing old *Survival Programs* that have become non-productive, negative, or even destructive, you only succeed in cementing the guarantee that nothing will ever change.

Many people have developed *Non-Survival Programs* which they continue to demonstrate even after they become aware of the problems those programs are creating (such as smoking, violence, unworthiness, shyness, arrogance, and so on). Whether conscious or unconscious, these programs sabotage personal and professional results. The negative results will continue until these behaviors are changed.

> If you always do what you've always done …
>
> you'll always get what you've always got.

In other words, if you want to ***get*** something different, you have to ***do*** something different. Unfortunately, the normal reaction to change is to resist it. Even when the old benefits are gone, the program often remains. Benjamin Franklin reportedly fought this tendency by changing a habit every 21 days. Interestingly, two centuries later, Maxwell Maltz showed in his book, *Psychocybernetics,* that it takes 21 day to change a habit.

Fortunately, we are not Sand Wasps. Human beings are probably the only creatures on Earth able to evaluate their circumstances and do things differently. Herein lies our ability to develop leadership excellence.

> *"Everyone thinks of changing the world,*
> *but no one thinks of changing himself."*
>
> … Leo Nikolaevich Tolstoy

Overcoming *Fear-Based* Reactions

You cannot overcome *Fear-Based* reactions, *Pre-Actions,* or *Non-Survival Programs*, unless you know they exist. On the other hand, you will not overcome them, unless you see them as a problem. Even then, you have to learn how.

> *"The definition of insanity is doing the same thing over and over and expecting different results."*
>
> … Benjamin Franklin

A middle-aged woman in a wheelchair told me the story of her crippling injury. She had been a high school teacher. During a fire drill, it was her job to see that everyone left the building as quickly as possible. A large student walked toward her, and she told him he needed to go outside. He said he wanted his jacket. Since it was not cold, she insisted he go outside and get his coat after the drill. The young man became so enraged that he picked her up and threw her against a wall of lockers.

Who knows for sure what caused this *Non-Survival* behavior, perhaps anger helped him to survive an abusive parent, but there was certainly some reason it developed. Apparently, he perceived the ability to intimidate people as valuable, even though it caused grave injury to them and ultimately put him in prison. Violent people might loathe the consequences of their behavior, but they continue to react with intense rage because of perceived benefits associated with the ability to intimidate or terrorize others.

Nonetheless, others use different techniques. In elementary school, I recall a girl struggling to answer a question from our teacher. Instead of answering, she began to tremble and cry. The teacher became visibly nervous and told her to sit down, where she continued to whimper. I cannot remember this girl ever being asked another question.

Falling apart had an immediate benefit for the young girl. She did not have to answer the question. It also had a long-term benefit. The teacher never called on her again. Shy people are not stupid. Even if they hate themselves for not speaking up, they often stay silent because of the inherent value in being able to avoid ridicule, rejection, or perhaps embarrassment.

These two young people had something in common with each other. Their *Fear-Based* reactions had become their ways of controlling others. The tough kid accomplished this with his Fight reaction, and the young girl with her Freeze reaction.

We have all known people who have learned to use the Facade reaction to control others with untruths, half-truths, and outright lies. Almost everyone has encountered Flight reactors who quit jobs if they think they are in trouble, or are always the one to initiate the break-up of a relationship.

> There are only two ways your life can improve …
>
> 1) Everyone else changes how they are treating you.
>
> 2) You change how you are treating them.

Our perceptions of the value of our *Fear-Based* reactions may blind us to the problems they are creating in our lives. We insist that others should do the changing, and go to great lengths to justify our own Fight, Flight, Freeze, and Facade reactions, even when they only serve to make things worse.

Your *Fear-Based* reactions usually do you harm, if only because they give others an excuse to react in turn. So even when you win you lose. People, who back off from your intimidation, may actively work to undermine you to get even. Your shyness may evoke kindness from those who care about you, but bosses who think you are too fragile to handle more responsibility may pass you over for a promotion.

It is normal to resist change, regardless of your desire not to do so. It is even harder to change those *Fear-Based* behaviors of which you are unconscious … even if they are ruining your life. A classic example is the practicing alcoholic who says, *"Drinking is not my problem. My crummy job is the problem."*

Knowing some of your own *Fear-Based* reactions will not guarantee you will increase your leadership effectiveness, but it is a vital first step. Take a minute to reflect on how you tend to react when you face challenges in life.

What is your primary *Fear-Based* reaction? What is your normal secondary reaction? Sometimes it helps to think about a recent situation where you feel some regret about your own reactions. Consider criticisms you have received from others. It is important to be honest here. Watch out for 'denial.'

While it is easy to categorize the reactions of other people, courage is needed for an honest self-evaluation. The following exercise will help you to get clear on your own primary and secondary *Fear-Based* reactions. Review the following four lists and circle everything you tend to demonstrate when things go wrong.

While everyone demonstrates all of these qualities from time to time, your results should at least give you a good idea which one or two *Fear-Based* reactions you tend to display most often. Your primary and secondary reactions will be the two with the highest numbers. Once you learn how to overcome your obvious *Fear-Based* reactions, it will become easier to deal with the more subtle ones.

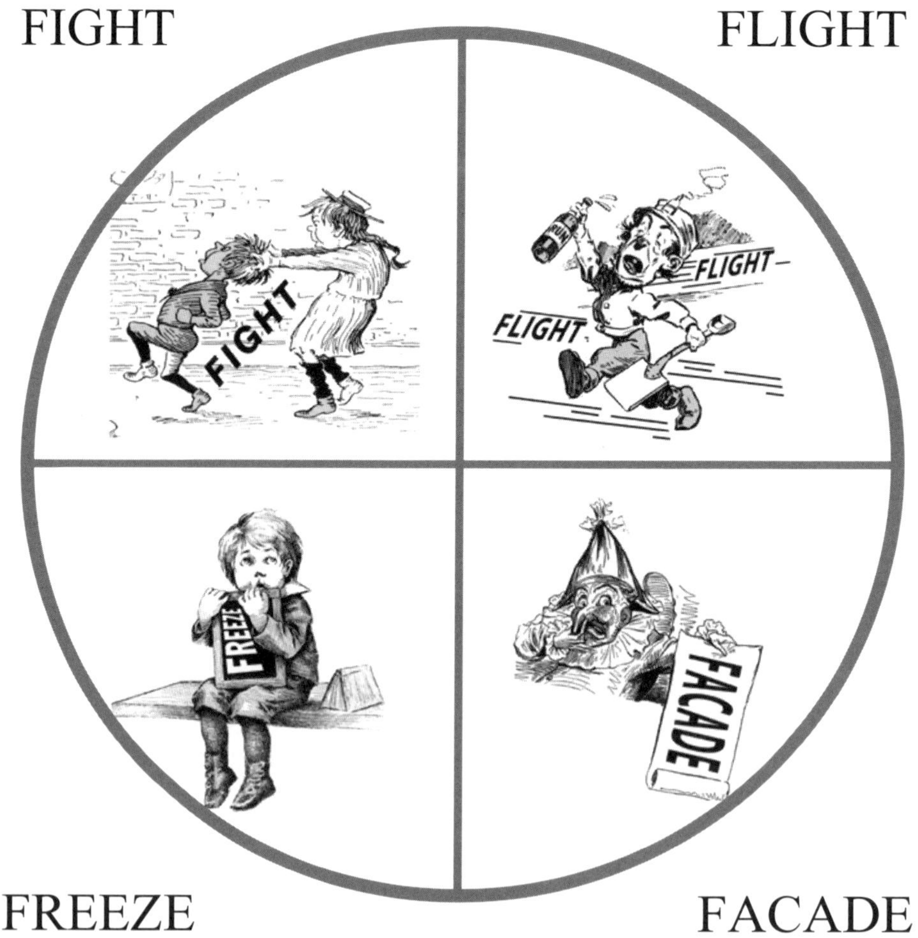

< SUGGESTION: Every time you come to an exercise, make a copy to work with>

EXERCISE

Circle Your Most Frequent Negative Reactions

List A	**List B**	**List C**	**List D**
Aggressive	Distracted	Anxious	Defensive
Argumentative	Excitable	Apprehensive	Fragile
Arrogant	Frantic	Inward	Guarded
Critical	Harried	Isolated	Guilt
Demanding	Hurried	Overwhelmed	Inferior
Intimidating	Hyperactive	Picky	Insecure
Insensitive	Impulsive	Serious	Intimidated
Judgmental	Overwhelming	Shameful	Needy
Manipulative	Panicked	Shut-Down	Phony
Offensive	Pushy	Tense	Subordinate
Sarcastic	Scattered	Withdrawn	Worried

Total the number of circled items in each column.

______	______	______	______
FIGHT	FLIGHT	FREEZE	FACADE

Your primary reactive program:
(pick only one) ____________________

Your secondary reactive program:
(pick another one) ____________________

Hints:

If you will not do this exercise, your primary reaction is probably FIGHT.

If you do all four reactions equally, your primary reaction is probably FLIGHT.

If you are stuck and cannot decide, your primary reaction is probably FREEZE.

If you worry about getting it right, your primary reaction is probably FACADE.

"Ross, when you react to your fear,
you do everything exactly wrong."

... My ski instructor in New Zealand

Chapter 2

Negative Reactions are *Fear-Based*

It is easy to be energized, loving, confident, and peaceful when everything is fine. The trick is to be able to do so when we are faced with unwanted challenges and negative circumstances.

> You do not need your mind to react …
> A mindless amoeba knows how to do that.
>
> **Stimulus … Response … Stimulus … Response**
>
> You only need one cell to react.
>
> *
>
> You need your mind to be able to choose NOT to react.

Unfortunate situations such as unemployment, harassment, crime, abuse, divorce, illness, accidents, injury, and death are unpleasant events we all must live with. However, they are not the problem. The problem is when they trigger your negative *Fear-Based* reactions.

Fear-Based reactions may take the form of white lies, manipulation, panic, nasty facial expressions, sarcasm, insincere agreements, shutting down, phony smiles, nervous laughter, jokes, or yelling. They can also be as severe as avoiding clients, quitting jobs, firing employees, dropping out of school, running away from home, divorce, child abuse, drunk driving, drug abuse, suicide, murder, or war.

It is important to remember that fear itself is not the problem. We all feel fear. It is a natural response to a threatening situation. It is our negative reactions to fear that create our problems. These reactions occur when you are either overwhelmed by fears of perceived threats, or as a direct result of having been in denial of your fears of real threats.

Overwhelmed by Fear

Fear-Based reactions can control your life, especially when they are triggered by 'perceived' threats. These reactions must be overcome for excellence to occur.

There is, for example, very little real danger when rock climbing if you are climbing with qualified individuals in accordance with generally recognized safety standards. In this case, if you fall, your spotters and the equipment will keep you safe. Whether you feel embarrassed or inadequate, you simply continue from where you fell, or try a different route.

Regardless, for many people **the fear of falling** creates a perception of danger that exceeds the possible benefits of successfully scaling a rock face. In such a case, otherwise capable persons give up before they start. They do not even give themselves a chance to experience this activity, never mind excel at it.

Similarly, when a salesperson slips and falls, and fails to make a sale, there is rarely unrecoverable damage. Rejection and frustration are simply part of the process. A successful salesperson simply goes on to the next prospect, learning from the experience and doing something differently.

For many people **the fear of rejection** creates a perception of danger that far exceeds the possible benefits of successfully making a sale. Just as in rock climbing, otherwise capable persons give up before they start. They do not even give themselves a chance to achieve excellence in sales.

In both cases, sales and rock climbing, when the perception of risk is grossly inflated, achievable objectives are not even attempted. In this event, 'playing it safe' guarantees failure.

> The main reason people
> do <u>not</u> have what they do want …
>
> They are too busy trying to <u>prevent</u> getting
> what they do <u>not</u> want.

The fear of rejection and the fear of falling are, for example, rational feelings. Rejection is painful, and falling could be deadly. There is a certain amount of wisdom involved in choosing behaviors which prevent you from being hurt. However, the cost of playing it safe can be enormous when the danger is only “perceived.”

When you do not make a sales presentation because you hate being turned down, you guarantee you will not earn a commission today. If you will not ask for a date because you are afraid of rejection, it is certain you will be alone tonight.

Thomas Edison did not create the light bulb by trying to prevent darkness, and you cannot create success by trying to avoid failure. You become successful by taking calculated risks, failing, learning from your mistakes, and giving it another shot … not by playing it safe.

> *“I've missed more than 9000 shots in my career.*
> *I've lost almost 300 games.*
> *26 times, I've been trusted to take the*
> *game-winning shot and missed.*
> *I've failed over and over and over again in my life.*
> *And that is why I succeed.”*
>
> … Michael Jordan

The answer is to develop the wisdom to identify perceived threats, and then to create the courage and determination to overcome your fears. While you will not succeed at everything you attempt, you will fail at everything you do NOT attempt. Failure is not the enemy, failing to overcome “perceived” threats is.

Denial of Fear

While fears of perceived threats must be overcome, fears of real threats must be addressed and dealt with. When you deny fear, and fail to be careful when facing a genuine risk, you place yourself in danger. When you behave without considering what might go wrong, you behave as a child who spontaneously runs into the street after a ball; disaster becomes a possibility.

> *"If I ever lose my fear completely ...*
> *I'll quit climbing."*
>
> ... My rock climbing instructor in Canada

When you deny your fears, you eliminate an important source of information when making decisions. You actually place yourself in harm's way, and set yourself up for *Fear-Based* reactions when things do go wrong. Denial represents the greatest danger to "fearless" people.

The macho guy, who does not see the risk of withholding his feelings, puts his fist through a wall when his girlfriend leaves him. The arrogant teenager, who does not appreciate the consequences of shoplifting, is mortified with the thought of phoning her parents after she has been arrested. The self-centered CEO is devastated when imprisoned for "cooking the books" for personal benefit. Many people, who drive as if they are immortal, have ruined other people's lives and their own self-worth after recklessly hurting or killing someone in a car accident.

The salesperson in the previous example erroneously plays it safe by avoiding appointments. The perceived danger of being rejected causes denial of the real risk of going broke. The real disaster happens when they lose a house or a job because of lack of sales.

The Two Keys To Excellence:

1) Risk when faced with a 'Perceived' threat.

2) Be very careful when faced with a 'Real' threat.

True wisdom lies in knowing which key to use.

Feelings

Feelings are internal signals that identify both positive and negative circumstances. While "good" feelings can lead you to wonderful experiences, and to quality personal and business relationships, "bad" feelings have value as well. You jerk your hand out of a fire because you do not like the feeling of your hand burning. This is precisely why the feeling of pain is valuable.

As such, feelings are neither good nor bad, they simply exist. Examples of feelings include hunger, irritation, joy, anger, pleasure, worry, serenity, nervousness, exhilaration, anxiety, happiness, resentment, **fear** and **longing.**

> *"Einstein found two fundamental forces motivating human beings ... fear and longing."*
>
> ... R. Buckminster Fuller

There is a constant battle between the feelings of fear and longing. Many people long for a successful career, but have an overwhelming fear of rejection, failure, or something else. For these people there will always be excuses instead of results, regardless of lofty goals or financial desperation.

Those whose longing for success is more important than their fears will do whatever is necessary ... in spite of their fears. This creates at least the chance for success.

Once, when selling advertising, I made a sale on a Friday afternoon. It was my best week ever. I was ecstatic. I knew my wife and my boss would be happy. I decided to reward myself by heading home a little early.

Then I thought, *"Why not make one more call?"* I turned the car around and saw a person whom I had been afraid would reject me. I figured, *"What have I got to lose?"* It turned out to be the single biggest sale of my career. His referrals made my next week even bigger.

Disaster can result when feelings are misinterpreted. Feelings of pleasure can lead people into the trap of drug addiction. Fear of rejection has prevented many from entering into beneficial relationships.

Emotions

To most people emotions are synonymous with feelings, but they are not. As previously discussed, feelings provide us with valuable information. Emotions, on the other hand, are how we pass this information along to others. It could be said they are the external evidence of our feelings.

Certainly, we can choose to emote our true feelings. Just as tears can be an honest expression of hurt, laughter can be an accurate demonstration of joy. However, both tears and laughter can be faked. What we choose to emote is influenced by our self-worth, beliefs, desires, experiences, and current objectives.

Emotions do not necessarily reflect or parallel our feelings. Examples include laughter, tears, frowns, smiles, prejudice, kindness, cowardice, courage, shyness, arrogance, forgiveness, vengeance, **hatred, and love**.

> We can choose to emote love, even when we have been hurt.
>
> We can choose to emote hate, even when we have not been.

Imagine you have just witnessed your child get hit by a car … not killed, but pinned under the car in great pain and terror. As you run to assist, you see an obviously drunk driver stumble out of the car. Simultaneously, you would be experiencing feelings of fear for your child, anger for the driver, and a longing for your child's survival. You would probably do one of two things:

1) Because of your feelings of fear and resentment, you would attack the drunk driver, get hysterical, shut-down, or run away.

2) In spite of your feelings of fear and resentment, but because of your longing for your child to be alright, you would choose to emote love. You would say things such as, *"I'm here," "Try to calm down,"* or *"You are going to be OK."*

Even though you CAN obviously emote love even when you have feelings of fear and resentment, you would probably choose NOT to do so for the drunk driver, (although some people may even choose to forgive later). Fear and longing, as with all feelings, are natural sensations. Love and hate, as with all emotions, while also natural … are decisions.

The Three Levels of Negative Circumstances

Despite the fact that all negative reactions are *Fear-Based*, fear is not the issue. Fear is valuable; it can keep us alive when there is danger. The real problem is the negative, non-productive, or destructive behaviors, which can be triggered by fear.

Negative circumstances do not cause *Fear-Based* reactions, but are used to justify them. When you react to being hurt, or pre-act to the possibility of being hurt, you actually blame others for your *Fear-Based* reactions. For example, *"I wouldn't have yelled at you if you hadn't yelled at me.*"

> The Three Levels of Negative Circumstances
>
> Level 1: DISTRACTION
>
> Level 2: DAMAGE
>
> Level 3: DEATH

Fear-Based reactions are always rationalized, even if afterwards you wish you had behaved differently. You may say, *"I can't believe I yelled at her,"* but you rationalized it anyway, perhaps because you were frustrated. At other times you might think, *"I should have ripped his lungs out,"* but you either justified withholding your anger to protect this person, or to protect yourself.

Negative circumstances do not cause *Fear-Based* reactions. If they did, we would all react in the same way when faced with a similar event, and we would do so every time. Yes, people have habits and tendencies, but nobody acts the same way all of the time.

Consider child abuse. It has been said that all child abusers have one thing in common … they were abused as children. Those who know the horror of it are the ones who pass it on to others. For these people, the problem has evolved from being abused **BY** others, to one of being abusive **TO** others.

Yet not all abused children become abusers. For some people, the negative circumstance of abuse has created new problems. They have become inward, fearful, shy, distant, and avoidant.

However, there is a third group. There are people who have been abused who have become neither abusive nor avoidant. These are the ones who strive to help others. Often, they become counselors for other victims of abuse. Sometimes, they even become counselors for abusers. I have met many such people. Their power is awesome.

As destructive as child abuse is, the circumstance of abuse is not the real issue for adult survivors. Their true problems are the *Fear-Based* reactions they have developed as a result of the abuse. Ultimately, it will be whether they choose to overcome these behaviors which will determine how successful they will become as adults.

> *"Suffering ceases to be suffering the moment it finds meaning."*
>
> … Friedrich Nietzsche

There are no guarantees. When you choose to strive for solutions to problems, others may still choose to react. If that is the case, however, you really have not lost anything. Anyone who reacts negatively to positive suggestions would have most likely been negative regardless of your actions. By taking the higher road, you create a chance for positive results, and those results can be amazing.

I have heard stories of hurt ranging from minor to deadly. Not surprisingly, the most intense reaction to hurtful situations is hatred. However, since hate is an intensely unpleasant emotion, many people will resist sharing or even acknowledging personal hurtful experiences. Unfortunately, just as a cancer you ignore remains deadly, the hate you bury is still destructive. This resistance to share prevents healing.

I have often said, *"However hurtful the event; hate is a choice. Hurt does not cause hate. You can make other choices."* Reactions to this statement have ranged from confusion to angry disbelief.

I have six children, and have been blessed to be present at each birth. During labor, I watched my wife's pain of childbirth increase to levels incomprehensible to me. However, when the big moment finally arrived, I observed a wave of peace followed by joy that still gives me shivers. I doubt any male can truly comprehend the experience.

If hurt caused hate, all mothers would loathe their newborns. In reality, many women go from agony to serenity just moments after giving birth. Most women would call the police if a man caused them one-tenth of the pain they experienced in childbirth, and they would resent him for decades.

"Now ladies," I ask my students, *"if a man were causing you this level of pain, would you be filled with joy and peace, just because he stopped?"* Of course not.

In childbirth, peace does not occur simply because the pain stops. Indeed, the pain often continues. There is peace because something significant was accomplished.

Conversely, suffering continues to be suffering if there is no meaning to it. *"If you hurt me just to hurt me, then you are evil, and I hate you!"* However, by hating, you suffer even more.

Many times I have said to a student, *"If you hate someone, who has the hate?"*

"I do," is the typical response.

Then I ask, *"What's that hate doing to you?"*

Many people have rationalized and avoided a truthful answer. Eventually, each would look at me and say, *"It's killing me, Ross."*

"There are three things extremely hard:
steel, a diamond, and to know one's self."

… Benjamin Franklin

Level-3 Negative Circumstance: DEATH

There is no circumstance more challenging to human beings than facing death. While some of us have more experiences with death than others, all of us will have at least our own death to deal with. Many people spend a lifetime in terror of dying. Nonetheless, if you are consumed with fears of death, you cannot truly live.

We are often overwhelmed with the passing of loved ones. We are also affected by the deaths of strangers, especially when it feels unjust. This was clearly demonstrated by the attacks on the World Trade Center and the Pentagon. Billions of people, not just friends, relatives, and acquaintances of the victims, felt a deep personal loss.

Level-3 negative circumstances often inspire *"eye-for-an-eye"* reactions, as well as possible escalations. One drive-by shooting is invariably followed by another. Convicted murderers may face the death penalty. A bombing in Northern Ireland only serves to justify a bloody retaliation. The United States invaded Afghanistan and Iraq following the attacks of September 11, 2001.

Leo Buscaglia ("Love 101" professor at the University of Southern California, hugging activist, PBS personality, and author of *Love*) viewed death as an inevitability, and said that we should stop being consumed with it and enjoy life. He used to joke about death in an attempt to reduce people's fear of it. At an address at the University of Illinois, he mused …

> *"We are trapped!*
> *None of us will ever get off this planet alive!"*
>
> … Leo Buscaglia

Level-2 Negative Circumstance: DAMAGE

Level-2 negative circumstances involve damage or destruction. Examples could include being passed over for a promotion, a house fire, a car accident, an audit, a mugging, having an idea stolen, breaking off an engagement, getting fired, going to jail, losing the value in a retirement account, getting a divorce, going bankrupt, or breaking an arm.

Fear-Based reactions to these difficulties often escalate them into even worse Level-2 negative circumstances. A salesperson gets drunk after losing a job, a car accident follows. A couple blaming each other for the unhappiness in their relationship may divorce. People have been known to get violent after a relationship break-up. Embezzle funds after being passed over for a promotion and you could lose your job or worse. Reacting to a Level-2 Negative Circumstance often makes a bad situation much worse.

> *"That which does not kill me makes me stronger."*
>
> … Friedrich Nietzsche

Regardless of how bad a Level-2 circumstance might be, at least you survived. Yet, many of us have seen people react so strongly that they have turned a Level-2 difficulty into a Level-3 disaster. A simple fender-bender triggers "road rage," which escalates into a fatal second collision. A disgruntled employee loses his job, then returns to shoot his boss, or other employees. In the Great Depression, some people committed suicide after losing their investments.

Level-1 Negative Circumstance: DISTRACTION

These are by far the most common negative circumstances. They include irritations, inconveniences, and unwanted surprises, such as having a bad waiter or being stuck in traffic. Other examples could include having a critical spouse, getting laughed at, having a bad hair day, missing a big sale, or your kids spilling milk.

Level-1 negative circumstances typically inspire similar Level-1 *Fear-Based* reactions. Glaring at people who cut you off on the freeway, yelling at someone who yells at you, or gossiping about someone who lied to you are three examples. However, Level-1 negative circumstances often motivate inappropriate and excessive *Fear-Based* reactions.

Have you ever gotten angry with someone who cut you off, because they just missed colliding with your car? In reality, they missed you. There was no accident (Level-2) and no one died (Level-3). Isn't NOT getting hit by another car a good thing? Yet, there are many stories of road rage escalating similar Level-1 negative circumstances into manslaughter (Level-3). They did not even need a fender-bender to justify it. *"You almost hit me"* was enough of an excuse.

> You are only as big as the smallest thing it takes to make you angry.

The Green Beret

Several years ago, there was a police officer in class who literally had no fears. Officer 'Smith,' a former Green Beret, was a member of his department's SWAT team. He could not relate to any *Fear-Based* discussions, except from the position of being able to see how other people reacted to him because of their fears.

Officer Smith told us of his dream to become a Secret Service Agent. In fact, everything in his life had been geared to that one goal for as long as he could remember.

Unfortunately, his dream was destroyed by one bad choice. While he was still in the army, he had been in a bar fight because someone offended his date. It turned into a 'Rambo' situation, with him ending up fighting the whole bar, and beating up several men. After his arrest, he found out that he had lost his security clearance, and his dream was now gone. There was no chance he could ever become a Secret Service Agent.

I listened to this story and when he finished, I took a breath and said to him, *"So basically, what you are telling me is that you are a weakling. You have no power, and it's probably a good thing that you didn't become a Secret Service Agent."*

I could see his rage building, but I continued. *"So let me get this straight. A guy said something you didn't like, so you had to make him pay for it. Let's see now, he spent an evening at the hospital, and you lost your dream. Who do you think paid the higher price? Who really lost?"*

His jaw slackened and he just looked at me, so I continued. *"You lost. You were beaten by sound waves. Basically, you were a wimp."* I have never been the type of person to quit when I was ahead.

I was slowly backing up at that point because I was pretty sure I would get a reaction. But, he just smiled and said, *"I understand. I think I'm getting it now. I've arrested people who've thrown their lives away because someone else made them mad. I always wondered how they could be so blind. Yet, I did exactly the same thing."*

I smiled and breathed a sigh of relief. He smiled again and said, *"You are the first person who has ever called me a name like that and walked away."*

I was truly grateful he understood what I was talking about. Had he attacked me, our fight would have been a joke. While he probably knew dozens of ways of killing someone, I have never even been in a fist-fight.

The Reactive Cycle

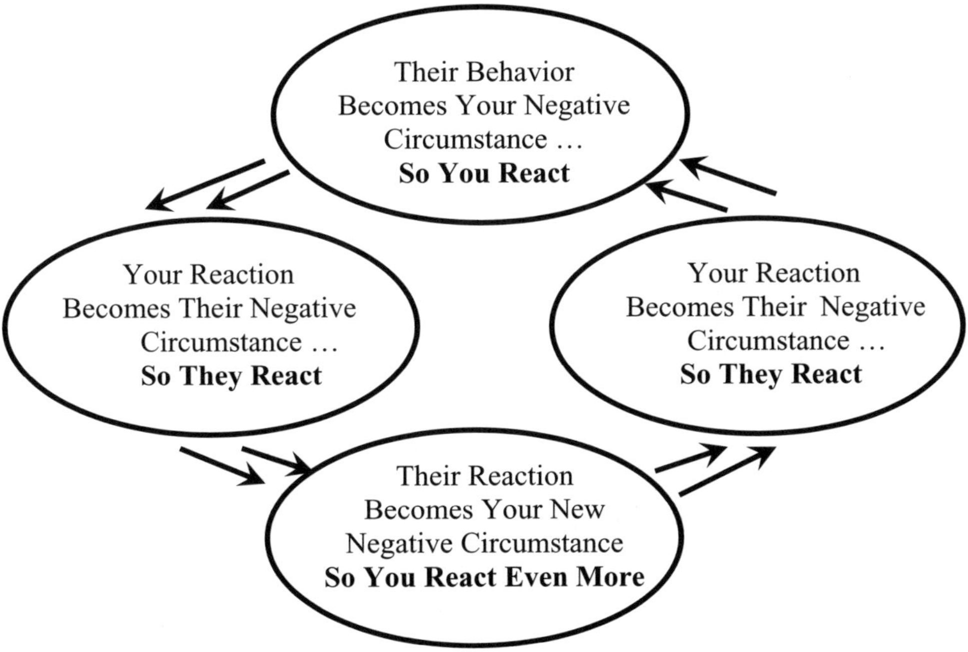

When you are in this cycle, and demonstrating any of the four *Fear-Based* reactions (Fight, Flight, Freeze, or Facade), you literally become a…

"***Victim of Circumstance***"

The Reactive Cycle

Whether overwhelmed by fears or in denial of fears, the real problem remains the same. It is not the negative circumstances that need addressing, but rather your *Fear-Based* reactions to them.

Your *Fear-Based* reactions become the negative circumstances for other people. You are reacting because they are reacting. They are reacting because you are reacting. Once begun, this cycle is extremely difficult to stop and in fact, it usually escalates.

Say you make the statement, *"I wouldn't have yelled at you, if you hadn't yelled at me."* Then the other person argues back, *"Well, I wouldn't have yelled at you, if you had kept your promise"* (or something similar). Justifications for *Fear-Based* reactions are easy to come by. When everyone blames everyone else for their own negativity, nobody is in charge.

Yet, while undesired situations often trigger your *Fear-Based* reactions, they do not cause them. Your negative circumstances are simply the excuses. They then become the excuses for other people's *Fear-Based* reactions in return. Once initiated, continued negativity accelerates this cycle.

The Three Stages of *Fear-Based* Reactions

First Stage .... RESENTMENT

Second Stage .... RESISTANCE

Third Stage .... REVENGE

Resentment

The First Stage of *Fear-Based* Reacting

Resentment is always present whenever a *Fear-Based* reaction occurs. Resentment is the first stage of reacting. You may resent others for controlling you, or for just attempting to control you, even when they tell you that they are doing so *"for your own good."* You may also resent others when you are unable to control them, even when you believe what you are doing is *"for their own good."*

> All acts of aggression and retaliation
> have <u>one</u> thing at their base …
>
> RESENTMENT

Yes, we resent people we hate. However, as anyone who has raised a child will verify, we also resent people we love. For this reason, people are often perplexed by their own feelings of resentment. However, as with all feelings, resentment has a purpose. You do not enjoy the feelings associated with resentment, but they do have value.

Again, imagine your hand is burning in a fire. Pain tells you to remove your hand before it is permanently damaged. Nobody enjoys the sensation of being burned. There is value in the pain, because it makes you respond quickly to avoid injury.

If you were to treat your burning hand the same way many people typically handle resentment in an argument, you would probably say something such as, *"Why should I move my hand? The fire should not be treating me this way. After all, I've given it the best years of my life!"* When your choices are based on resentment, you become a *Fear-Based* reactor, and you risk injuring yourself as well as others.

Alternatives such as forgiveness are easiest to implement in the first stage of reacting. Failure to do so is a decision to proceed to the second stage of reacting. Unfortunately, because *Fear-Based* reactions tend to escalate the scale of damage, solutions become progressively more difficult to implement at each stage.

Resistance
The Second Stage of *Fear-Based* Reacting

After Resentment comes Resistance. Do not confuse caution with resistance. Caution is necessary for survival. Resistance, on the other hand, is a signal you are no longer in control of yourself or your destiny, and that the choices you are making are ultimately not in your best interest. Resistance is self-destructive and does nothing to create self-worth, quality relationships, or business success.

Resistance can be expressed in many ways. Shy people resist sharing, even if they hate themselves for not speaking up. Angry people resist being patient and giving love, despite the fact the people they care about are being pushed away. Battered women resist leaving abusive husbands while living in terror. Frightened people resist new relationships, even when they loathe being alone.

> What is the normal reaction to change?
>
> RESISTANCE
>
> (Even if what you are doing is not working)

It is obvious that resistance to removing your hand, when you feel pain in a fire, would be destructive to your hand. What is not so obvious is that resistance to changing your behavior, when you feel resentment in an argument, is just as destructive to yourself and your relationships. Pain and resentment are feelings intended to inform you of danger. Resistance to these signals can be disastrous.

Sometimes, you justify your resistance to expressing hurt or anger because you do not wish to upset people whom you care about, or whom you fear. *"After all,"* you may rationalize, *"it was really not a big deal,"* and you repress your negative feelings.

Eventually, however, these feelings will become stronger than your resistance to showing them. As difficult as it can be to overcome resistance in order to implement positive alternatives, it is far easier than attempting to do so at the third and final stage.

Revenge

The Third Stage of *Fear-Based* Reacting

After Resentment comes Resistance. Unless a conscious choice is made at that point, Revenge (the Third Stage of Reacting) becomes inevitable.

Revenge comes with a built in irony. While it targets others in an attempt to get-back-at, get-even-with, or get-away-from them … revenge carries elements of self-sabotage, or even self-destruction, as we develop emotional reactions, *Pre-Actions*, and programs of hatred. In fact, revenge by us can easily become more damaging than what is done to us.

> *"When you hurt someone else, you hurt yourself a lot worse."*
>
> … Your Grandmother

As with resistance, revenge can take many different forms. Theft, sabotage, divorce, abuse, ridicule, destruction of property, and murder are but a few examples. People have even been known to destroy themselves with drugs and suicide, in order to hurt someone else.

Vengeance targets people you hate, such as those who have abused you or a loved one. Other examples could be a friend who let you down, a former boss, your ex-spouse, the 'other' man or woman, or a thief.

Revenge can also be directed at people whom you care about. You might spank a child for embarrassing you or gossip about a co-worker who got 'your' promotion.

When you blame your negative behaviors on another person, destruction will ultimately result. Your reaction becomes the other person's negative circumstance, which increases the chances for them to react (again). When you react often enough, eventually your negative behaviors will not even need a trigger to occur.

George's Story

The names are fictitious, but the following story is true. It works best if you imagine the story is actually happening to you, so pretend your name is George (yes, women too).

About 25 years ago a friend of yours, Bob, started a company in Thousand Oaks, California. He was the president and majority stockholder. David, the vice-president, was the financial backer and held most of the remaining shares. You were hired as the plant manager and were given a small share in the company. Bob promised, *"George, you will be taken care of when the business succeeds."*

Even though your salary is less, and you have fewer shares than the other partners do, you consider this your company. You have worked days, evenings, weekends, and even on holidays when needed.

Because of the teamwork, friendship, and abilities of the three partners, the company has become a profitable business employing over 200 people. This is one of those companies from which people never quit, and are rarely fired. It is a big event whenever there is a marriage, birth, or retirement. It is more like a family than a business.

One day David tells you he is retiring. A little later, you get a note from the boss …

George,

I need to meet with you at 9:00 tomorrow morning. We have something very important to discuss.

Bob

What goes through your mind, George? Something like, *"Twenty-five years and finally I will get the promotion I deserve."* You are certain that you will get a raise and probably a larger share of the company.

Of course, you cannot wait to tell your wife the good news. You get home a little early to tell her, and she almost bursts with joy. She exclaims, *"We've waited so long for this!"*

Your wife tells you the beautiful home you have dreamed of owning is up for sale. This house is on a hillside with a beautiful swimming pool and a great view of the entire valley. With a larger salary, plus the equity in your home, you will surely qualify for a loan. All evening your excitement grows.

You get very little sleep that night, and your wife fixes you a wonderful breakfast in the morning. As you leave for work you hear her say, *"Don't forget to call."* You can see the excitement on her face. You love her and appreciate her support so much. You could never have done this without her.

You get to your office full of anticipation, and go to the boss's office early. You are waiting as he enters. *"Good morning, George, come on in,"* and he tells his secretary to hold all calls.

"As you know," he begins, *"David is retiring and we need to replace him. George, I want you to be the first to know that I'm bringing my cousin Horace from Toronto to be the new vice-president. I need you to teach him the business."*

Remember, this is a true story. How would you feel if this were happening to you? The blood rushes from your head. The words you just heard are not possible. *"I need you to teach him the business,"* keeps running through your mind. *"I don't understand,"* you blurt out.

"George, I need to hire Horace in this position and you're the one person I can count on to make sure he is properly trained. I need you to do this."

"Bob," you plead. *"What's going on here?"*

He replies, *"I can't get into it now. Don't worry; I'll take care of you."*

"I'll take care of you." You hear the words screaming in your head. *"I've heard that before."* You leave his office in a daze.

You are full of resentment, aren't you?

Who are you resenting, George? The Boss? Horace? David? Perhaps you are even resenting yourself? Then you suddenly think, *"Oh my God, my wife. This will crush her."*

Negative thoughts are racing through your head. *"Twenty-five years. He promised me. How can he treat me like this?"* The resentment keeps building. *"I made this company for him! He's gotten rich off of me. He's taken vacations I could never afford. This is the thanks I get? I trusted him."*

Do you call your wife? Not likely. You move from resentment to resistance. You resist calling your wife. You resist working. You just sit at your desk, suffering ... until you head for a bar. Finally, about 2:00 a.m., you come home.

Your wife has been waiting all day for your phone call about the promotion. You come home late, drunk, and angry. You tell her the "good news" about Horace. How does she react?

"How can you let them treat you like this?" She shouts. Your wife resents Bob, Horace, and especially you. She is even resenting herself for supporting you all of these years. She storms off to the bedroom. You sleep on the couch, and fix yourself cold cereal for breakfast.

You arrive late for work. Resistance has begun. *"After all, I've worked weekends, nights, and even holidays for his company. I've earned a late morning, and then some."* Bob introduces you to Horace, and asks you to take him around the plant to meet everyone.

Do you build Horace up to the employees? Or do you sabotage him?

"This is Horace, our new vice-president," you tell them. *"He is going to make our company work."* You wink and give a smirk to these people who are your close friends. Your resentment and resistance is spreading to others. Now your co-workers are also angry and resentful because you were not promoted.

> *Fear-Based* reactors focus on the reason for their reaction, rather than on the fact they are reacting.

Upon returning to the office, you are introduced to Horace's wife. She and the boss's wife have been house hunting all morning. *"Horace, you'll never believe the house we found,"* she gushes. *"It's a beautiful home up in the hills, with a swimming pool and a breathtaking view."*

"My God," you think. *"They're buying our dream house. If my wife finds out about this..."* and you cannot even finish this thought because of your fear of her reactions. More resentment builds within you.

She continues, *"Bob has agreed to help us with the down payment. Let's go see it and make an offer right now!"* That is about all you can stand, George. You finally break. Now it's time for revenge.

You take a little money out of petty cash and take off for the racetrack. *"I've earned it,"* you justify. *"Besides, I'll pay it back. They owe me a chance to win a little money."* Of course, you lose it all.

Your resistance is intensifying. You spend almost no energy training Horace, but a great deal of time in the plant with your friends, venting your anger at the boss and putting Horace down. Otherwise, you are losing at the track almost every day.

Two weeks later, your thefts are discovered when the president calls for a surprise audit of the books. Sadly, Bob has no choice but to fire you from the only job you ever loved.

But your tribulations are not over, George. Not long after you are fired, your wife leaves you. So now, not only did you lose your job and your marriage, you lost your house in the divorce. Eventually, you go bankrupt, become an alcoholic, and die alone and bitter.

However, there is one thing you never knew. Bob could not bring himself to tell you or anyone else he had just found out he was dying of cancer. He was consumed with two things, the survival of his company and the financial needs of his wife.

He believed that if news of his condition reached his customers, they might lose confidence and shift to a different supplier. Bob also thought if the company were sold, his loyal employees might lose their jobs. He decided to hide the truth (the Freeze and Facade reactions), and devised a scheme.

First, Bob bought back David's shares in the company and persuaded him to retire. Next, he arranged for Horace to become the new vice-president. Bob wanted Horace to learn the business from you because, in return for your many years of loyal service and friendship, he was going to give you the company. You were to become the president and owner.

Bob knew you would run the company properly and that the employees would gladly work for you. The only condition would be for you to share the profits with his wife for as long as she lived. They had no children. Bob felt he could trust you, and that you deserved to be the president and owner.

However, because of your justified resentment, you lost it all. Not long after you were fired, the boss died. Horace was incapable of running the company, and since he had no support from the employees, it went out of business. Two hundred people lost their jobs. The shares Bob was going to give you were instead left to his wife. They became worthless. Your behavior hurt your wife, the boss's wife, and hundreds of your friends, co-workers, and customers.

Who loses when you choose resentment? EVERYONE.

EXERCISE

Non-Survival Programs, by definition, are unconscious behaviors. Changing them is impossible, unless you discover what they are. Here are two ways you can uncover your *Non-Survival* Programs:

1) Have you ever done something, regretted it … but later did it again?
List a few examples:

2) Have you avoided doing something, regretted it … but when given another chance avoided it again? List a few examples.

PART TWO

Four E's of Excellence

Results Not Excuses

ETHICS

FACADE

The result of most *Fear-Based* attempts at communication, is **'misunderstanding.'**

Chapter 3

Ethics – The Alternative to the Facade Reaction

The Facade reaction occurs when you are overly concerned for the feelings of others, and lie to protect them. It also happens when you feel intimidated and lie to protect yourself. Either way, because you tell people what you feel they can handle or what you think they want to hear, Ethics is sacrificed and your comments will be untrue: *"You look fine in that dress;" "I'm sorry;" "I'll do whatever you want;"* or *"I can change."*

Often, people do not say what they are truly thinking, but end up hurt or angry when they are misunderstood. When you are worried, your primary concern is to evade problems and conflict, but your truth suffers. Unfortunately, your Facade reaction provides justification of Fight, Flight, Freeze, or Facade reactions in return. It may delay, but does not prevent, the Reactive Cycle.

> *"Clarity at all costs ... or it costs you all."*
>
> ... Christine G. Quinn (my wife)

A typical Facade reaction is to fake agreement, to 'keep the peace,' which may have the opposite effect. Unless your intention is to have others react to you with negativity, you need to make a conscious choice to eliminate any perception that you could be lying.

Perhaps your intention is to be kind and supportive, but because you are 'walking on eggshells,' it can appear to others as if you are being insincere. If this behavior threatens them, and it often does, they will react to you. You, in turn, react to their reaction and the Reactive Cycle escalates.

To overcome the Facade reaction, your feelings can guide you to share your true thoughts and feelings. This is especially important when doing so would seem likely to cause difficulties. 'Biting your tongue' solves nothing, and tends to create new problems.

When you make a ‘boldfaced lie’ intended to hurt someone, resentment invariably results. However, even a ‘white lie’ designed to benefit another often creates problems.

If your relationship is important, share the truth with kindness. Be direct in saying what you need or want, without filtering anything. Remember that the Facade reaction, even when motivated by good intentions, is a lie.

> Whether you lie to protect someone else or yourself, you may temporarily achieve desired results …
>
> but the lie will eventually come home to haunt you.

Whether you remember it or not, you would not be using the Facade reaction unless you had experienced being hurt when you tried to be honest. You might have been punished for being truthful. Maybe you shared a great idea, but were ridiculed by friends. Perhaps you were blunt, and hurt someone’s feelings … or even lost a friendship.

Eventually, you developed the Facade as one of your defense systems. Perhaps feigning agreement kept people off your back. Pretending to love may have made you feel that you were being kind to someone you knew you were going to hurt with an eventual break-up. Providing misinformation to others may have allowed you to have a scapegoat when something went wrong. You may have concluded that acting nice is what made people like you. Regardless of the reasons, your Facade reactions had to have had some value for them to become habits.

"Sarge"

My father's mother, Lydia, had lived with us since I was a child. Her husband passed away from cancer shortly after my birth. Having someone with her strength and experience was fortunate for my parents.

Even though a large woman, Gram's power was in her indomitable spirit. Everyone called her "Gram," not just family. However, my brother and I nick-named her "Sarge" because she was so strong-willed. I have never met anyone with a greater love of people, or with less fear of rejection.

"Sarge" raised three successful sons … Paul, James, and Charles. In her lifetime, she also taught school, ran a ranch, managed a fabric store, was in charge of enrollments for our LifeStream seminars, and traveled extensively. At her passing, Gram's wake attracted hundreds of people. As a measure of her impact, almost half of those in attendance had never even met her.

When Gram was about 80, my mother began to notice she was emanating a body odor, even though her personal hygiene habits apparently had not changed. It kept getting worse and worse. Mom said nothing about it, as she did not want to hurt Gram's feelings.

My mother casually started to question her. *"Have you changed your soap?" "Have you started wearing a new perfume?" "Are you using a new deodorant?"* Each time, Gram would respond that nothing had changed.

Finally, it got so bad my mother overcame her fears of hurting Gram's feelings and told her how offensive her odor was becoming. Gram was shocked, but not embarrassed. Nothing embarrassed her. Together they eliminated all possible causes of the odor, and decided to have it checked out by her doctor.

Testing confirmed cervical cancer. Surgery and treatment successfully took care of the problem. However, her doctor told them it could have been fatal had they waited much longer. It was very close. To this day, I remember my mother's lament; *"Gram almost died because I was worried about hurting her feelings."*

Fear-Based Facade reactions always involve a lie.
Even the act of sparing someone's feelings
can have terrible results.

Ethics

Ethics could be defined as the alignment of vision and behavior. The excellent leader behaves in a manner consistent with their ideals. He or she can develop trust, because promises are kept and results are achieved.

> Consciously choose to make what you say will happen ... happen.

The ethical salesperson says, *"I will exceed my goals,"* and will do whatever it takes to do so morally and legally. He or she will overcome all obstacles. If it means calling on twice as many prospects to achieve a goal, then that is what will happen. If a family emergency comes up it will be handled. Afterwards, it is back to work with an even higher resolve. Intentions equal results.

However, many unsuccessful salespeople lack ethics. These people will set goals they do not believe in to pacify or to impress a boss or a spouse. By setting pie-in-the-sky goals, there will be two results…

1) They will fail because any obstacle will beat them.

2) This failure will not be their fault. They will have a good excuse, ending with a phrase that will sound something like, *"Besides, it wasn't really my goal, it was my manager's."*

'Victim' stories are just excuses. Murphy's Law, *"If something can go wrong, it will go wrong,"* only provides unethical people with victim stories. Results take effort.

At the core of ethics is honesty. Speak your truth, but do not kid yourself. People are your barometer. If people are reacting negatively to you, your idea of ethics is probably much like the proverbial 'Bull in a China Shop. It is possible to be honest and compassionate at the same time.

Ethics begin with doing or sharing something worthwhile, and then acknowledging yourself. It develops by noticing how others respond. If results are not forthcoming, an ethical leader will change what they are doing. If others react, they will overcome their own *Fear-Based* reactions and change <u>how</u> they are expressing themselves (not just by getting louder), until others get the point.

Speak the other person's language. If you are harsh with someone who needs understanding, you might as well be speaking Greek to a German … they will not hear you.

The Facade reaction is *Fear-Based*. 'White Lies' are justified in order to spare the feelings of others. Blatant lies can find their base in fears of poverty, rejection, abandonment, looking stupid, and so on. There is no limit to the rationale available for the Facade reaction.

The ethical leader is not dependent on the approval of others. He or she knows when something worthwhile has been accomplished, even if everyone else decries or ignores the achievement. Decisions are made because they are in alignment with personal vision, not because they are popular. Whatever the "job" is, the focus is upon "getting the job done." The following quote is often misunderstood, and is generally taken out of context…

> *"Winning isn't everything. Winning is the only thing."*
>
> … Coach Vince Lombardi

However, Coach Lombardi's interpretation of 'winning' changes the meaning of this famous statement. According to Bart Starr, his two-time Super Bowl champion quarterback, people rarely asked for Lombardi's definition of winning …

> *"Never go out to beat the other guy.*
> *Only go out to be the best you can be. Then, you are winning."*
>
> … Bart Starr (quoting Vince Lombardi)

The Problem … Your "FACADE" Reaction

When demonstrating Facade reactions, you strive to make things look better than they really are. Whether you are trying to protect yourself or someone else, you say only what you think others can handle … or what you feel they want to hear.

You will ask yourself or others **"Why"** types of questions …
*"**Why** me?" … "**Why** can't we just get along?"*
*"Nothing's wrong, **why** do you ask?"*

When You Are Consumed With FEELINGS and EMOTIONS,
Your Primary Characteristic Tends to Be WORRIED

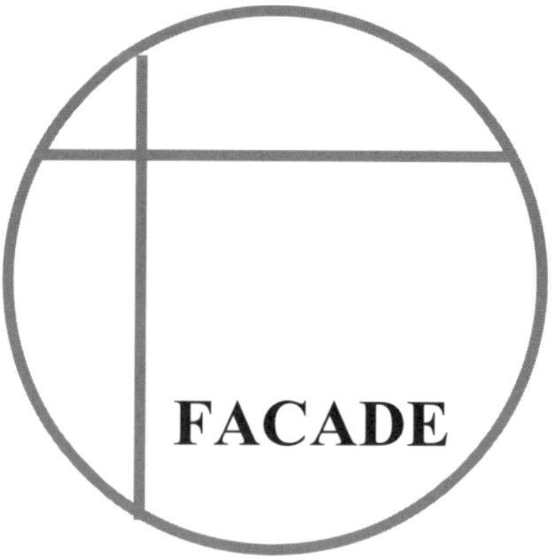

I say one thing to your face, but I'm thinking something else.
Out loud, *"I'm fine. I'm just fine."* Inside, *"I'm hurt and angry."*
Out loud, *"I'll buy your product."* Inside, *"I'll cancel tomorrow."*

Other Characteristics:

Intimidated	Defensive	Phony	Subordinate	Guarded
Guilty	Insecure	Inferior	Fragile	Needy

The extreme Facade reaction is to become DEPENDENT

The Solution … Add ETHICS

Be congruent by saying what you really mean. Tell people WHAT is happening (not why), and/or WHAT you are going to do. You need to risk rejection, give others assurances, and let people know what you are truly thinking and feeling. Never let your emotions, feelings, or issues get in the way of creating "Desired Results."

> *"Never mind if people don't understand you, so long as no one misunderstands you."*
>
> … R. Buckminster Fuller

Balance Yourself by Focusing on …

ETHICS

Choose to become …

Accountable	Thorough	Bold	Efficient	Decisive
Determined	Congruent	Focused	Honest	Confident

Become RESULTS Orientated

The Tool: Creating "Desired Results"

Most people avoid setting goals. There is a simple reason for this. When you set a goal and fail, you feel bad. The solution for many people, instead of learning from the experience, is to stop setting goals. It is a little like the old joke, where a patient says, *"Doctor, it hurts when I do this,"* as he raises his arm over his head. The doctor replies, *"Then don't do that."* So, we won't do that here.

NO MORE "GOAL SETTING"

From now on use only the terminology … Creating "Desired Results." It may sound like semantics, and perhaps it is. However, sometimes it is just a matter of changing perspective a bit, in order to get our brains to cooperate. Open your mind and test out this technique. You will not be disappointed. There are only 7 guidelines for creating desired results.

Guidelines for Creating "Desired Results"

They need to be …

1. Important, Challenging, and Positive
2. Achievable
3. Specific, Time Sensitive "Events"
4. Written Down, and Shared
5. Visualized Daily, BEFORE Going to Sleep
6. Balanced
7. Celebrate Victories and Failures

Guidelines for Creating "Desired Results"

1. Important, Challenging, and Positive

If your desired results are not important to you, the smallest obstacle will prevent their achievement. If you do not "own" them, which is usually the case when they are chosen by someone else, your commitment will be lacking. You must have a passion for your desired results. Make them important and own them … or do not bother with this.

Your desired results should be challenging. Beating the odds creates huge levels of satisfaction, and makes further successes more likely. Desired results, which are unchallenging, will not create a sense of victory when achieved. Beating someone at a game they have never played, for example, has little satisfaction.

Keep your desired results positive. A 210-pound person should be striving to weigh 199 pounds, not to lose 11 pounds. Focus on what you DO want, not on what you DO NOT want.

2. Achievable

Do not set desired results that are too high. If failure seems imminent, denial and avoidance may follow. Start small, and keep your desired results simple. As you achieve them, set higher ones. Even if you only add slightly to your previous victories, you will continue to grow and win. It is important that you acknowledge all progress.

If you have not read a book in 10 years, starting with something by Tolstoy will ensure frustration. Start with something short, like Jonathan Livingston Seagull. If you have not exercised in 20 years, a desired result to run in a marathon may not be healthy. Start with a training regimin to get you to where you can first complete a 5K run.

Weight loss is a special category. You did not gain the extra 50 pounds in 2 months, so do not try to lose them in 2 months. I recommend between 4 and 10 pounds a month. Know your limits. Slow and steady wins this race.

3. Specific, Time Sensitive "Events"

If your desired results are vague, such as "I will make more money," they will never create a sense of victory. Specific targets are best, especially when they are TIME sensitive. *"I will sell $1,000,000 worth of widgets this year"* is an excellent example.

A desired result should be an "Event," such as completing a marathon or exceeding your quota. "Activities," such as running every day or calling on more customers, are necessary, but not the focus here. This technique is concerned on the "What," not on the "How."

4. Written Down, and Shared

This is so simple, but most people avoid it. Write down your desired results where you can see them on a daily basis.

As soon as you have chosen a desired result, show it to someone. If possible, make an agreement with that person to challenge you periodically on your progress. Pick someone who will support you, someone who has no stake in the outcome, and who will not buy into your excuses.

5. Visualized Daily, BEFORE Going To Sleep

Perhaps the most important element of creating desired results is to use your mind at night. Before getting ready for bed, find a comfortable place to sit. Do NOT do this lying down in bed, because you may fall asleep. Turn off the TV and, if possible, play symphonic music.

Close your eyes and visualize a structure … a workshop. This is an imaginary place, where you go to create desired results. Inside this workshop is a huge TV, covering an entire wall. This is the "Screen of Your Mind."

Every night, visualize your desired results on the TV screen. See them as if they had been achieved earlier in the day. Then, imagine how you would feel. Play a "Back-to-the-Future" mind-game with yourself. Make the feelings as real as possible.

When you are finished, prepare for bed. While you are falling asleep, let your mind contemplate the feelings you would have had … if you had created each of your desired results earlier that day.

As you gain proficiency, your mind will provide you with insights and solutions as you need them. Keep a journal or tape-recorder beside your bed, and make note of any insights or ideas you receive throughout the night.

6. Balanced

For balance, always have four desired results; one physical, one emotional, one mental, and one spiritual. Replace each desired result as it is achieved.

Physical: These are desires to improve your health, appearance, energy, diet, fitness, calmness, or are just to pamper yourself. Achieving a desired result of weight-loss, becoming smoke-free, competing in a 5K walk/run, or completing a marathon are typical. Other examples include getting a physical exam, dental exam, manicure, massage, facial, or pedicure.

Emotional: These are desires to improve an important relationship (intimate, personal, social, family, or business). It is something that will be done WITH that person, not FOR them. Having a family outing, or going on a date are typical. Other examples include phoning an old friend, having lunch with a parent, taking a get-away weekend, or having an intimate dinner with your spouse. Remember, this must be something the ***other*** person would enjoy or wants to accomplish … perhaps something you have been avoiding.

Mental: These are desires to improve your self-esteem, knowledge, career, prosperity, or are just for pure fun (remember "*All work and no play makes Jack a dull boy and Jane a dull girl.*"). Getting a promotion, completing a degree program, or achieving a big sale, are typical. Other examples include reading a book, taking a course, going hot air ballooning, cleaning the garage, or finishing a project.

Spiritual: These are desires to give of yourself to others, to become significant, or to make a difference. Donating money or volunteering time at a place of worship are typical. Other examples include things such as donating clothes or furniture to a women's shelter, reading to a shut-in, giving blood, picking up litter, or joining the church choir.

7. Celebrate Victories <u>and</u> Failures

Celebrate your victories, no matter how small. However, the most important step in Creating "Desired Results" is to also celebrate your failures. By looking for something to learn from each failure, you increase your chances of future successes. That is worth celebrating.

The Fired Banker

"Ralph" was a banker in a major metropolis. He made a mistake and was fired. After several unsuccessful attempts to get a new job in banking, he came to me for advice. I told him, *"While banking is a large industry in this city, it is a small fraternity. Everyone knows what happened to you. Realistically, you either need to change careers, or move to a different city."* I thought this was a reasonable strategy.

Ralph disagreed, saying, *"My wife's family is here, and I don't want to leave banking."* He had drawn his line in the sand, so to speak. Now I had to help him come up with a solution.

First, I said, *"Let's start at the beginning. Clearly, by trying to say the right things to prospective employers, you are coming across as insecure and phony. You need to start using the power of your mind to overcome your insecurities. Tell me, how will it feel to finally get past all these problems and land a good job?"*

Ralph replied, *"It will be a relief. I will be excited. My wife will be ecstatic."*

"OK. Here's what I want you to do." I continued, *"Before going to bed at night, visualize yourself shaking the hand of someone who has just offered you the job you want … and create those feelings of relief and excitement."*

"Nope," he responded. *"I have a better picture. Your father has always said that the mental picture must be exciting. Sure it will make me feel good to get back in banking, but what really excites me is the thought of finally getting a Porsche."*

I thought he was kidding. He was not. Nothing I could say would dissuade him. Finally, Ralph said, *"Look Ross, for me to get a Porsche, I will have to have a hell of a job."* With this, I relented and helped him create his mental picture.

"Close your eyes and imagine yourself walking up to your brand new Porsche." He let out an audible sigh of pleasure. *"Now smell the interior. Sit on the leather seats. Adjust the mirror. Most importantly, I want you to notice how you are feeling."*

"Perfect," he responded with a grin.

"Turn on the engine and hear the sound. Feel the sensation as you begin to drive. Notice people turning to look." He was grinning ear to ear.

"That's it," I finally said. *"Do this every night until it is in your garage. I have never seen it fail. Remember, you have to create this mental picture and the resulting feeling … AS IF IT WERE REAL … every night until it happens. No matter how long it takes."*

"I'll do it," was Ralph's reply.

Less than three weeks later, he had his job. His employers agreed to finance his new car. It was a beauty. By using his mind before going to sleep, Ralph was able to change his attitude and thinking so he could interview from strength instead of desperation. This empowered him to land the job of his dreams.

The power of the human mind is beyond measure. By using your mind at night to visualize your desired results, you too can manifest your goals and dreams. It always works.

> Ethics is about being accountable, honest, and results oriented.

Creating 'Desired Results' is a learned art. Use the following 'Exercise' to get started. Long-Term effectiveness will come with practice. Stick with it and you will find profound value in learning and using this tool.

EXERCISE

Pick four (4) "Desired Results" and follow the preceding guidelines. Then replace each one as it is achieved. By starting with short-term "Desired Results" (to be achieved within 30 days) you will make it much easier to have, and celebrate, victories.

Physical:____

____

____

Date To Be Completed: ________________

Emotional:_______________________________________

____

____

Date To Be Completed: ________________

Mental:____

____

____

Date To Be Completed: ________________

Spiritual:____

____

____

Date To Be Completed: ________________

"Live one day at a time …
emphasizing ***ethics*** *rather than rules."*
… Dr. Wayne W. Dyer

"The first step in the evolution of ***ethics*** *is …*
solidarity with other human beings"
… Dr. Albert Schweitzer

"Non-violence leads to the highest ***ethics****,*
which is the goal of all evolution"
... Thomas Edison

BOTTOM LINE

When worried, risk failure, but speak your truth.

Focus on behaviors which ASSURE others
you can be counted on to achieve Desired Results.
Somehow, some way, you will get the job done.

ETHICS

What you think, what you say, and what you do …
are all the same.

Seriousness is a Curable Disease

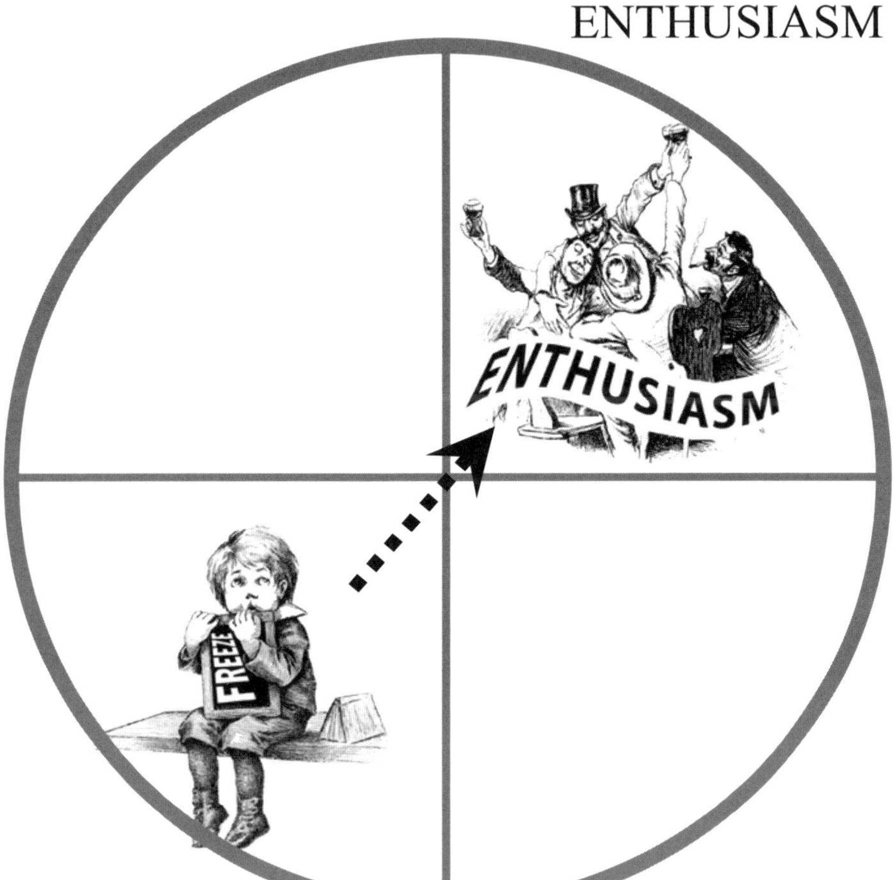

"The only thing more contagious than Enthusiasm is the LACK of it." … James H. Quinn

Chapter 4

Enthusiasm – The Alternative to the Freeze Reaction

When stress triggers your Freeze reaction, you bite your tongue, hide in your "cave," shut down, or become unresponsive. In extreme cases, denial of love makes you shut everyone out. You will not share your real thoughts or feelings until you have figured everything out, or are certain it is safe to do so. While the Freeze reaction is often an attempt at self-protection, this behavior is sometimes a conscious choice designed to protect others.

When you are shutting down, other people may or may not be your primary concern. You may be interested in sorting out your own thoughts, or you could be trying to protect someone else. Unfortunately, the Freeze reaction can be threatening to others, because they have no way of knowing what is really going on with you. They have to guess, and their assumptions can be much worse than the reality of whatever it is you are trying to hide.

> The FREEZE *Fear-Based* reaction often occurs with people who feel they are overwhelmed.
> Unfortunately, this can trigger impatience from others.

Someone who tends to become analyzing, distant, or isolated, can be perceived as annoying or boring. This can lead others to exhibit *Fear-Based* reactions, such as attacking, shutting down, running away, or lying.

People may react to you even if you just appear to be isolating. Perhaps you are not really shutting down or shutting them out, but are so focused on solving a problem they feel ignored or taken for granted. If someone feels threatened they will react to you and the cycle will escalate. The problem you are hiding from only grows larger as you hope, in vain, that it will go away. Most of us take ourselves much too seriously when we are in the Freeze reaction, and therefore procrastinate when faced with challenges. Spontaneity is missing.

> The great masters never said, *"Seriousness to the world."*
> It was always, *"Joy to the world."*

The question becomes*, "How can I move into Enthusiasm, when I am in the middle of a Freeze reaction?"* The answer is; tell people exactly how you are feeling and what you are thinking, before you figure out exactly what to say. In other words, learn to 'think-out-loud.'

Since the extreme Freeze reaction is to become Avoidant, the choice to come from Enthusiasm seems rash or even dangerous. This is difficult to argue with, because the Freeze reaction has one purpose … self-protection. Whether you remember it or not, you could not use the Freeze reaction unless you had the experience of being embarrassed or put-down when you were excited about something or someone. When you were spontaneous, you might have been told to "shut-up." There may have been a time you were told, *"What will the neighbors think?"* Perhaps you were teased or bullied, and found safety by staying invisible. Regardless of your reasons, you must have perceived value in the exhibition of Freeze reactions in order for this behavior to become a habit.

However secure it feels, the Freeze reaction is still *Fear-Based.* Inappropriate people and challenging circumstances trigger your "head in the sand," or "nose to the grindstone" approaches to problems. You are only happy when circumstances are perfect, and they are never perfect. Bottom line, you give up control of your life when circumstances are in charge of your behavior.

Just as a deer freezes in the headlights of an oncoming car, you are in danger when you analyze yourself into immobility. To place yourself in this kind of "voluntary" solitary confinement is to treat yourself as you would the very worst of criminals. There is an element of self-punishment involved when you isolate with the Freeze reaction.

You do not have to be alone to Freeze … most of us have done so in a crowded room. In personal relationships, one person may interpret a lack of enthusiasm from their partner as a lack of affection. When someone feels rejected, unloved, or taken for granted, they may feel they have no choice but to look for another partner for warmth, attention, and affection. Destructive affairs and divorces can result, as it is more fun to be with exciting people.

Likewise, business relationships require enthusiasm and interaction in order to prosper. In business, timely information is often more desirable than perfect information (for example, imagine the following dialog preceding a battle, *"Sergeant, send a message to the general that the enemy is advancing from the west, not the south."* ... *"No, Captain. Not until I can tell him exactly how many troops."*). In a business world that moves at "Internet" speed, delays can be fatal.

It is rare to find only one correct solution to a problem or challenge. Success in business often requires assumptions, risk, and enthusiasm.

> When tempted to Freeze,
> take your power back with Enthusiasm.
>
> Realize you are probably avoiding when you get
> 'Paralysis of the Analysis.'

Enthusiasm

If you do not have enthusiasm, not much else matters. To live with enthusiasm is to have the energy to enjoy life. The personal rewards of living enthusiastically can be great. Problems become opportunities to create joy. Even daily exercise can become fun.

The effect of enthusiasm on others is, perhaps, more significant. An unenthusiastic speech or sales-presentation is boring, regardless of the importance of its content. Conversely, even a poor speech has some impact when delivered with enthusiasm.

One of my favorite moments from a leadership seminar occurred when a dyslexic student took up a challenge to deliver a speech. No amount of practicing was helping. In fact, the more he worked on it, the worse his condition became.

I watched him fumble with sections of the speech he had already learned. I tried to help, but he became so frustrated he literally had trouble remembering his name. Finally, I told him as long as he was certain he was going to screw it up, he might as well do so with enthusiasm. Have some fun with it. After all, I told him, *"They pay Jim Carrey about $20,000,000 a movie to act dumb. Perhaps being perfect is not all it is cracked up to be."*

He thanked me and said he would make it fun. I was not certain if he was going to pull this off. Nonetheless, he was determined to give it his best shot.

However, from the moment he began, I knew it was going to be a wonderful speech. He had decided to change the beginning so the audience would understand what he was going through. He started with a joke.

"Have you heard of the new organization called DAM," he began. *"It stands for Mother's Against Dyslexia."* I could not believe it. This serious, self-conscious man was actually making fun of his disorder.

His speech was titled "Courage," and was written by William Penn Patrick after he failed to become the Republican candidate in the 1966 race for the Governor of California (he lost to Ronald Reagan). Honestly, of the dozens of times I have heard it delivered, I have never seen it messed up so badly. Nonetheless, his speech was one of the best I have ever seen.

We were not laughing at him, we were laughing with him. He also made us cry. People hung on his every word, even when he had to try the same sentence several times. The courage he showed far exceeded the courage he spoke of. His points got made, people understood his message, and we all had some fun.

In this story, it is important to note that even though this "serious" man did not eliminate his dyslexia or his terror, he was able to create enthusiasm and deliver his message in spite of that fact. He was entertaining and informative, and as motivational as you can get.

Certainly, enthusiasm alone is not enough. However, when those in leadership positions try to "motivate the troops," they had better do so enthusiastically. Without it, no amount of logic, threats, or pleading will be effective. Not only do such efforts usually fail, they often seem to create even bigger problems.

> There is little point in having a purpose in life,
> if you cannot have fun fulfilling it.

Leaders, by definition, have followers. People are your barometer. Excellence is evident when you attract people who support, befriend, love, or endorse you. However, when people are not drawn to you, you might as well be pushing them away.

An "Autistic" Adult?

Some people are clear about their strengths and weaknesses, yet may still benefit from looking deeper to find gifts yet to be discovered and developed. Those with low self-esteem need to realize that they actually have value. Often, their gifts can be found "amongst the ruins" of some incredibly challenging life-circumstances.

> *"There is not anyone who cannot in some way add to Universe and contribute to humanity."*
>
> ... R. Buckminster Fuller

When I first met Jane, she could not look anyone in the eye. She was in her own little world, and nothing I could do could get her out of it. I began to wonder if there was such a thing as an autistic adult.

It took some doing, but after two days of hard work, she was finally able to converse with other students while actually looking at them. It was like watching a rose begin to blossom. Jane began to sport a lovely smile.

Then I told the group we were going to examine our childhoods to discover a few of our gifts. *"Some of your higher qualities have been squashed, and you have longed for their return. Others, you may not even know about,"* I said. At this point, Jane crossed her arms and legs again, and stared at the floor.

"What's up Jane?" I asked. Then I asked it twice more before I got a response.

"Nothing," She said without lifting her eyes.

"Come on Jane, please look at me and tell us what is going on," I asked.

Reluctantly, she looked at me and said, *"I cannot do what you are asking. I had an awful childhood, and I can't bear to think about it."*

"Okay, so what was it like?" I seldom leave well enough alone. She looked away and did not answer.

"Tell me why you are so shut down. What was it like?" I repeated. Jane just stared off into space.

"If you will not even talk about it, then there is nothing to be accomplished here. I have to ask you to leave the class." While I did not

want Jane to leave, I felt if she did not take a leap of faith now, it would matter little if she stayed.

Jane glared at me and said, *"You don't understand. I'm dying inside. I can't leave."*

"Fine. Then tell me why you are so shut down?" I responded.

Jane said, *"Because I can't, and I won't."*

"Then you have to leave the class." I replied.

"I can't leave. I need this class. I am dying." Jane was pleading now.

"Then tell me why you are so shut down." I repeated.

"You don't understand. I have been in therapy for 10 years. My therapist has never gotten me to talk about my childhood, and you expect me to talk about it? Just like that?" She was shouting.

"Yes," was my reply. So she did. Jane began to open up.

She told us of a childhood of isolation and sexual abuse. I will not go into the details, but it was the worst story of childhood abuse and neglect that I had ever heard. Basically, she was either ignored or molested. Jane remembered little else.

She was never praised, hugged, nurtured, or given a present of any sort. Jane was even ignored on her birthdays. In fact, she told us, *"The only thing I had to play with was a doll I made out of a few sticks and some rags. That doll was the only one I could talk to. That's how sick my childhood was. I finally left home at 15. No one even cared about that."*

"How wonderful," I responded. My tone was not sarcastic, but gentle. I was filled with admiration.

Jane did not understand, however, and asked, *"What's wonderful about that?"*

I said, *"You were treated as nothing. You were used, hurt, and isolated. Given the same circumstances, I doubt if I would have been as strong. I would have probably just wallowed in self-pity. But, you chose to do something about it. You made a doll so you could have a friend. That is powerful. Tell me, what did you name her?"*

She was shocked, *"How did you know I named her?"*

"Simple," I replied. *"Nobody with your courage and determination would NOT name the doll. How wonderful that you didn't kill yourself to escape your life of pain. Not only that, you left home and educated yourself. You have a good job, a nice home, and have spent 10 years in therapy trying to find your self. Jane, you have greatness."*

Jane looked at me and smiled. Had I asked her to define her best qualities, courage, determination, and most certainly, greatness would not have been among her responses, but they were obvious to me.

After the two hours it had taken to get through this sharing, Jane was ready for anything. Talking about the rest of her life was easy. She had always dreamed of having a husband, but feared abandonment. She desperately longed for children, but feared her own childhood would become their destiny.

Jane also had ideas for her own business. Unfortunately, her feelings of unworthiness and fear of rejection had prevented her from making it a reality.

Talking about her childhood did not eliminate its pain. Jane was still terrified of others, but became the class leader in spite of her fears. Living her life under a bushel basket had kept her safe, but it had suffocated her. Jane simply made a decision not to live that way any more. From that time onward, she was the first to share, quickest to question, and was always willing to challenge others. It was a remarkable transformation.

I do not always see the end results of my seminars, but it is particularly gratifying to hear from people who have completely turned their lives around. Five years later, Jane wrote to me.

The letter spoke of my challenge for her to quit wallowing in self-pity and to do something with her life. Jane said that after class she entered and graduated from a business college, and then met and married a wonderful man. Not only that, her life-long dream of having a child had been fulfilled.

I went on to read that this terrified and unworthy woman had also created her own successful business. If I live to be a thousand, I will never forget her closing words …

… Finally, I promised myself I would write you when I felt successful. Well, yesterday I hired my 100th employee, and I want you to know how successful I feel.

Thank you for believing in me.

Love, Jane

The Problem … Your "FREEZE" Reaction

When demonstrating Freeze reactions, you become analyzing, isolated, and generally avoid others. Whether you are trying to get something right, figure something out, or are avoiding a relationship, you do not even speak until you have had the time to collect your thoughts.

You will hear yourself internally asking **"How"** types of questions....
*"**How** can you say that to me?" … "**How** can I do all of this?"*

When You Are Consumed With TASKS,
Your Primary Characteristic Tends to Be OVERWHELMED

"I don't want to talk about it."
"In the time it takes to explain, I can do it myself."
"If you can't say something nice, don't say anything at all."

Other Characteristics:

Anxious	Inward	Picky	Withdrawn	Apprehensive
Serious	Shameful	Tense	Isolated	Shut-Down

The extreme Freeze reaction is to become AVOIDANT

The Solution … Add ENTHUSIASM

Make something happen. Focus on WHO to spend time with and WHEN you need to do so. You probably need to play, give others your full attention, and let people "in" to your world. Quit worrying about HOW everything will work out. Planning your spontaneity can help remove some of the unknowns.

> There is no problem you can have,
> which you can't make worse … alone.

Balance Yourself by Focusing on …

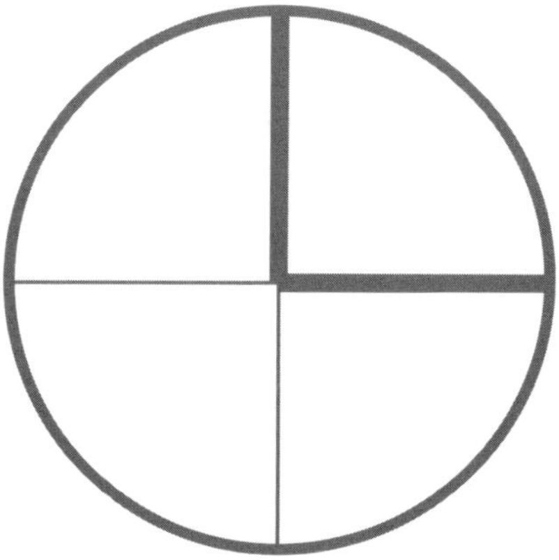

Choose to become …

Spontaneous	Energetic	Promoting	Open	Expressive
Positive	Exciting	Creative	Stimulating	Persuasive

Make TIME for RELATIONSHIPS

The Tool: Planned Spontaneity

Adherence to the old adage, *"Look before you leap"* has saved many people from making terrible decisions. The problem with the Freeze reaction is becoming too analyzing. Yes, action without thinking can be dangerous, but thinking without action is nearly pointless. Sometimes, it is okay if everything is not perfect.

> Occasionally, spontaneity is necessary.
> Every now and then you need to get a little crazy,
> or you will go nuts.

One of my more analytical students came up with a solution, which worked well for him. Everything in this man's life was planned. His wife was originally attracted to him because of his stability. Now she was beginning to see him as boring, and he was resenting her for trying to have fun with him when he was busy. He knew this was not smart, but could not bring himself to change.

He was in danger of losing the only woman he had ever loved. Try as he might, his projects always had to be finished before he could relax and enjoy himself. Since completing projects was not his strong suit, and starting new projects was never a problem, there was never any point of completion.

Then a solution occurred to him. He decided to treat his wife with the same energy as a project. He knew what she needed was some occasional fun, so he began to plan spontaneous fun things to do with her. That's right, "Planned Spontaneity."

He actually scheduled time to be spontaneous. It sounded ridiculous, but it worked. Since he was impeccable with his appointments, once he booked some play time with his wife, it became a priority. He stopped resisting her.

Here is how it worked. At the beginning of the week, he would find a couple of hours of open time and book it as if it were a business appointment. Then, he would think about what kind of event he would create. He might plan to take his wife to a movie at a nearby theatre, go for a walk, or visit some friends. Once it was entered in his weekly planner, he could let it go.

When the scheduled time arrived, he would find his wife and tell her he wanted to take her to a movie. Whatever was showing was what they saw.

Sure, they saw some movies they hated, but sometimes they discovered a film they really loved and would never have seen.

This began to work so well, he decided to start creating fun in another way. This stiff, serious man began to teach himself how to juggle. After a while he became pretty good at it. Eventually, he began to teach others to juggle. Now, when he finds himself in a long line, he starts to juggle, and usually makes new friends.

Their marriage has healed. He is still a workaholic, but the fun is always present. Sometimes, he surprises his wife with a flower, dinner at a new restaurant, or even an unplanned trip. Of course, when he is in the supermarket, there is always fruit to juggle. His wife never knows what to expect. There is no longer any danger of her thinking of him as boring.

EXERCISE

Plan an hour of spontaneity. Book it into your Palm Pilot or weekly planner. This must be something fun ... and you must take someone with you.

Journal the experience:

"You can do anything if you have enthusiasm."
... Henry Ford

"Nothing great was ever achieved without enthusiasm"
... Ralph Waldo Emerson

"Enthusiasm is a vital element toward the individual success of every man or woman"
...Conrad Hilton

BOTTOM LINE

When overwhelmed, instead of shutting down,
do something Spontaneous with another or others ...

even if you have to plan it in advance.

ENTHUSIASM

Always remember, without movement you stagnate.

Mistakes are Learning Experiences

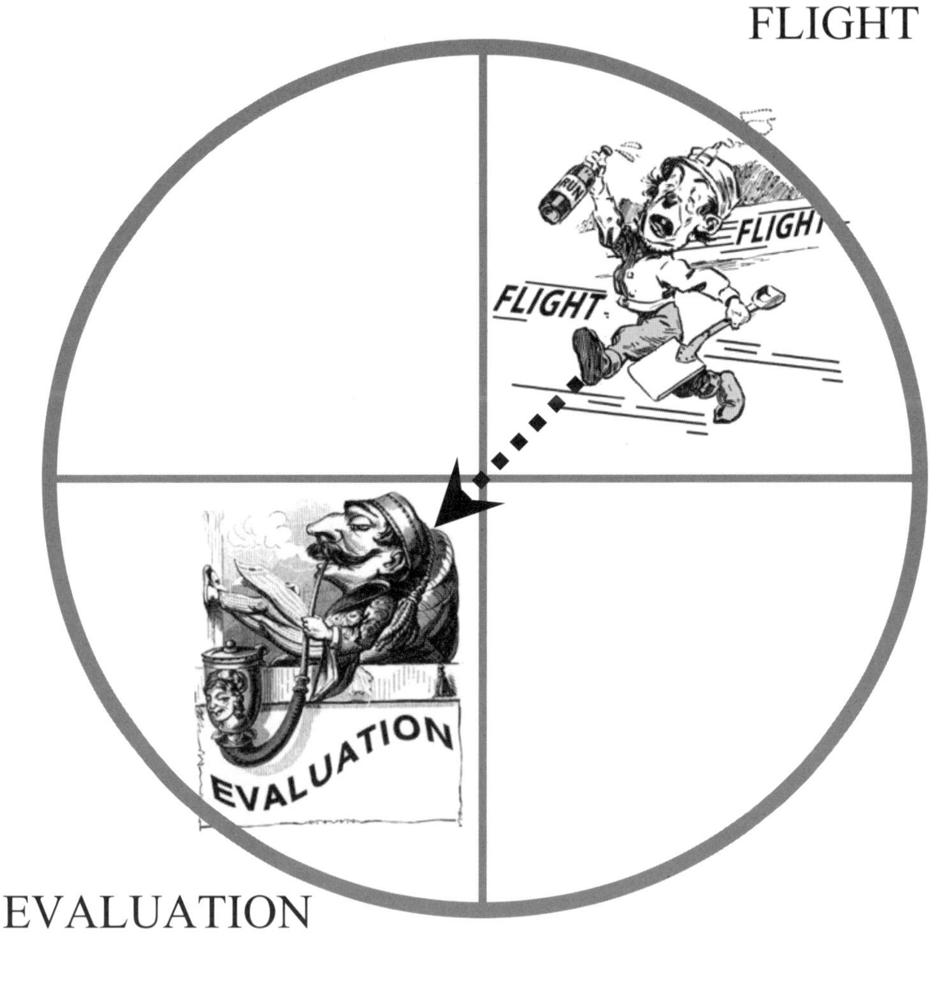

"Learning isn't a means to an end; it is an end in itself"
... Robert A. Heinlein

Chapter 5

Evaluation – The Alternative to the Flight Reaction

Sometimes we find it impossible to face challenging situations, so we run from them. Flight can take many different forms such as quitting a job, firing an employee, ending a friendship, or divorcing a spouse. Sometimes it manifests in the form of "running off at the mouth."

When you are in the Flight mode, you may make comments such as: *"I can't talk now"; "I'll take care of it later"; "It's not my fault I'm late;"* or *"Forget the plan, I have an idea."* When you get frantic, other people's plans, goals, or needs are not your primary concern. You feel as though you are painted into a corner and are only interested in getting out. Unfortunately, your Flight reaction often provides justification for the Reactive Cycle to begin or accelerate with others.

If you know someone who is chronically late, then you know that ignoring or avoiding problems does not make them go away, it only makes them worse when they finally catch up with you. Problems cannot improve if they are not addressed. The Flight reaction practically guarantees disruption and chaos in the lives of others, who will then point to your behavior as their justification for attacking, shutting down, running away, or lying to you.

> The faster I go … The 'behinder' I get.

People may react to you even if you just appear to be frantic. Perhaps you are firmly dug into your "Enthusiasm" mode. Not frazzled, but so intent on your problems that others feel unappreciated, used, or walked-on. If this threatens someone, it will begin the Reactive Cycle. They will react to you and then you react to them.

We have been taught to learn from our mistakes. Unfortunately, for most people mistakes are <u>not</u> learning experiences, because they repeat non-productive, negative, and even destructive behaviors, hoping that there will be a different outcome.

The human mind is quite possibly the most incredible creation in the universe. It allows us to evaluate our actions and make changes to our behaviors, in order to create beneficial results. Unfortunately, people will never find personal or business success as long as their mind-set is on scarcity, luck, status-quo, unworthiness, insecurity, or any number of other issues. Self-evaluation and the willingness to change are vital characteristics for personal and professional development.

Evaluation begins with determination. You have to know that, somehow, you will become a successful salesperson, a good parent, a great manager, or a happy spouse. Failure and mistakes are not the problem. The problem is repeating them. The solution is learning from your mistakes, and doing something different the next time.

The best salespeople have one thing in common: after each sales call, whether successful or unsuccessful, they review their performance. These people evaluate the good and the bad to find things deserving acknowledgement, as well as to find things to improve.

If you want to **GET** something different, you must **DO** something different. Overcoming issues and learning from mistakes requires a mind-set for self-improvement. Without honest self-evaluation, the power of your mind will be reduced to rationalizing your own behaviors. Nothing will change. Your answers require a determination to grow.

> *"People are a lot like fruit.*
> *When they're green, they grow.*
> *When they're ripe, they rot."*
>
> ... Bernard Beruce
> (Also the motto of Ray Kroc)

It has been said that monkeys can be captured by placing a piece of fruit in a jar which is tied down. When the monkey reaches his hand into the jar, he discovers he cannot get his hand back out without dropping his prize. Instead of letting go of the fruit and running away as humans approach, he clings to it until he loses his freedom.

Most people are willing to try to make a job or marriage work, but really do not change what they are doing. They cling to behaviors that have already proven to be ineffective.

Reportedly, Thomas Edison tried thousands of experiments before his incandescent bulb actually worked. Notice, he tried thousands of DIFFERENT experiments. If Edison had repeated only the same experiment he would have been passed over by history. We all need to evaluate and learn from our failures in order to grow.

Ideas for evaluation typically come from taking an objective look at your self, considering both the positive and negative feedback from others. One very effective way to do this is to take the time to journal a couple of paragraphs of observations, feelings, and insights at the end of each day. Afterwards, meditate on what you have written.

Without taking the time to reflect on potential solutions and keeping your priorities straight, you may hurry to an appointment, quit a job, or divorce a spouse in an attempt to avoid stress. Unfortunately, if your peace of mind is controlled by a circumstance, changing or controlling your circumstance only provides a temporary solution.

Lasting answers are to be found by changing yourself. When stressed, calm down and do things differently than normal.

Evaluation

When you find yourself frantically trying to accomplish more than can possibly be done, you may actually be fleeing from your problems instead of facing them. Here is a simple way to change that pattern. The next time you find yourself in crisis mode, stop and reflect on the reason you made a commitment, started a job, agreed to a project, or entered a relationship. Those desires or needs are probably going to go unfulfilled if you break your integrity, and you will eventually find yourself in the same frantic position in the next circumstance or relationship.

> *"Every time I left a marriage, everything I was running from got to the next relationship before I did."*
>
> … A former student after her 4th divorce.

Since the extreme Flight reaction is to become histrionic, the choice to come from Evaluation seems impossible, and is resisted because of the immediate time crunch. This is difficult to argue with, because the Flight reaction has one purpose … self-protection.

When confronted with problems, you would naturally tend toward Evaluation unless you have found some value in the Flight reaction. Perhaps by being frantic, you became difficult to pin down and, therefore, difficult to call on the carpet for broken agreements. Perhaps you found it easier to walk away from challenges and problems rather than face them. Others may have started solving your problems when you went into panic mode.

Whatever the reason, the Flight reaction exhibits *Fear-Based* living. If you choose to cling to this reaction, you are allowing other people to determine your peace. Unless you find a way to change, you will continue to react frantically when stressed. Begin by examining how you can keep your word or how to create what you originally wanted. Take the time to make plans. Make major changes slowly and with great consideration. Stop and prioritize what is important, and then finish one thing at a time … especially when it seems impossible to do so.

The Real Estate Salesman

Jim was usually the first person to arrive in his real estate office. This was a good thing since he always seemed to be behind in his paperwork. This morning he was meeting with a new client.

Bob spoke slowly and had difficulty describing the property he wished to purchase. Jim kept probing and questioning in an attempt to find out what this guy wanted, hardly waiting for Bob to finish his sentences. When the meeting was over, they made an appointment to go look at properties the next day after lunch.

That night, Jim poured over his Multiple-Listings book (this story takes place in the pre-computer era). He identified six different properties he felt would please his client.

The next day Jim had a long lunch with the local merchants association. He did the best he could, but got to his office 20 minutes late for his appointment. Bob was not disturbed by his lateness, but seemed eager to get started. Jim, on the other hand, was already thinking ahead to his next commitment to meet with another client in two hours. They had to hurry if Bob wished to see all the properties.

At the first stop, Jim knew he was in trouble. Bob slowly wandered through the house examining everything in minute detail. His slow drawl was beginning to frustrate Jim. Finally, after unsuccessfully showing all six houses, they got back to the office. Jim found his next appointment waiting impatiently for him.

He made another appointment with Bob. This time Jim made the appointment his last of the day, so it would not get in the way of other clients. Jim stayed up later than usual, selecting eight more properties from his Multiple-Listing book.

True to form, and after an exhausting morning, Bob still had not found the home he was looking for. After five meetings, and four days of looking at homes, was about to cut his losses and tell Bob to work with another realtor. That is when he called me.

I suggested Jim give Bob his Multiple-Listing book, and let him take it home to study overnight. Back then, in the era before the Internet, the Multiple-Listing book was not supposed to leave the realtor's office. Jim resisted this idea until he realized he had nothing to lose by giving it a try.

The next day Jim said, *"Bob, instead of running all over town again today, I'd like you to take my Multiple-Listing book home. I want you to look through it and see if you can find something I've been missing."* Bob's eyes lit up like a Christmas tree.

The following morning, Jim came into the office to find Bob waiting. He had found the perfect home and did not want to wait for someone else to get it first. Jim was a little perplexed. The home Bob had chosen was quite a bit more expensive than the upper limit he had been given. Jim would have already shown this home if he had known.

As they visited the property, Bob was as excited as a child opening presents. Everything was perfect and the sale closed quickly. It was one of Jim's largest sales of the year.

By taking the time to let Bob evaluate his own needs and desires, Jim allowed Bob to answer all of his own questions and objections in his own time. As a result, Jim never quite got around to the Flight reaction (dumping one prospect in favor of a better one).

Remember, when you are about to employ the Flight reaction, come from Evaluation instead. The answer, when frantic, is to stop and clear your mind. Your priorities will become clear and you will generally save more time than you had feared you might lose.

The Problem … Your "FLIGHT" Reaction

When demonstrating Flight reactions, you panic, make excuses, rush, "motor-mouth," or interrupt others. Whether you are trying to find something for someone, make it to an appointment, or get away from someone, you say the first thing that comes to your mind. You are not listening to anyone else.

You will hear yourself asking **"Who or When"** types of questions …
*"**Who** do you think you are?" … "**When** is my appointment?"*

When You Are Consumed With a RELATIONSHIP(S),
Your Primary Characteristic Tends to Be FRANTIC

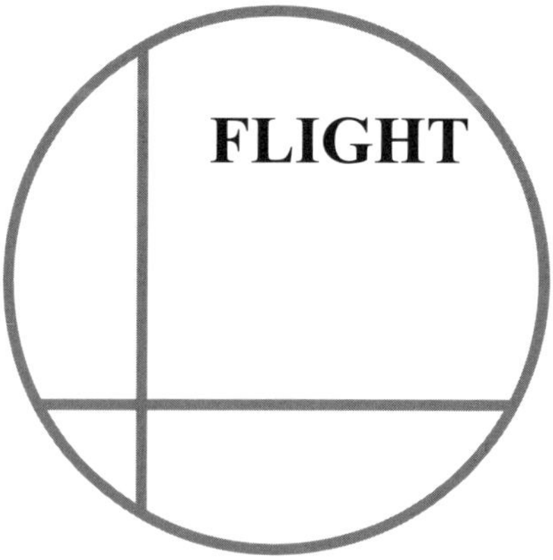

"I don't have to take this, I'm out of here."
"Don't worry about it … I'll take care of it later."
"I've got too much to do and not enough time to do it."

Other Characteristics:

Distracted	Overwhelming	Harried	Panicked	Hyperactive
Impulsive	Hurried	Excitable	Pushy	Scattered

The extreme Flight reaction is to become HISTRIONIC

The Solution … Add EVALUATION

Solicit ideas and feedback, and actually consider what you hear. Take the time to figure out HOW you created this stress, and HOW to prevent it in the future. You need to slow down, give others information, and let others help you. Remember the moral from Aesop's Fable, *The Tortoise and the Hare … "Slow and steady wins the race."*

> *"My life works in direct proportion*
> *to the commitments I make and keep."*
>
> … James H. Quinn

Balance Yourself by Focusing on …

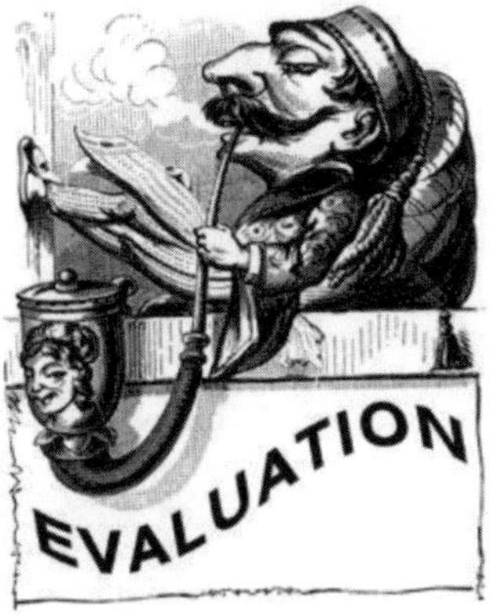

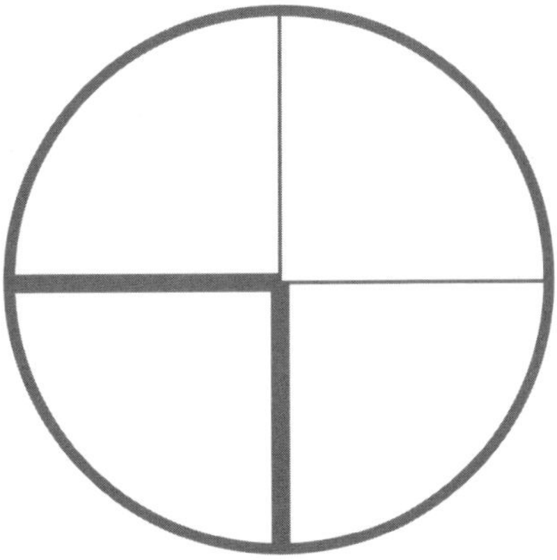

Choose to become …

Patient	Diligent	Reliable	Industrious	Methodical
Detailed	Persistent	Integral	Precise	Deliberate

Focus on TASKS and COMMITMENTS

The Tool: Centering

The reduction, 're-direction,' or elimination of stress is essential in the modern world. There are many ways to accomplish this objective. Examples include exercises (such as Tai Chi or Aerobics), hobbies (building models or reading), and meditations (Transcendental Meditation or centering).

Almost any discipline is effective, as long as it gets your mind off your troubles. Two things which do NOT work are 1) becoming consumed with your problems, or 2) avoiding them with drugs, alcohol, shopping, food, work-a-holism, or escapist activities.

> With meditation, as with exercise, you should learn the techniques from a trained professional who can guide you through the intricacies and nuances of their respective systems. They can also adapt their techniques to fit your special conditions or circumstances.

I practice and teach a safe, simple, and effective "Centering" technique. This powerful tool aids people in stress reduction and self-discovery. Centering involves meditating on the seven colors of the rainbow.

For optimum results, center from 5 to 15 minutes every morning. I suggest you do this AFTER getting up, as learning this technique in bed can put you back to sleep.

During the day, in periods of high stress, even one or two minutes of centering can be highly beneficial. Quiet spots may be hard to come by, but there are restrooms almost everywhere (seriously).

Practice centering every day for 21 days. It will begin to feel as natural as brushing your teeth, putting on make-up, or shaving.

EXERCISE

Preparation:

Follow the general outline below. Most people find it beneficial to make a recording based on this outline. Soft, symphonic music, or sounds from nature will help create a supportive environment.

Sit with your feet flat on the floor. Move your feet slightly forward so your ankles are directly beneath your knees. Open your palms, as if you are holding a huge beach ball on your lap. Lift your chin so that your eyes are elevated slightly above the horizon. Push your shoulders back and straighten your spine.

If you prefer to lie down, position yourself as follows to maximize your results and prevent yourself from falling asleep: Lay on the floor, not on your bed (old sleep patterns are difficult to beat). Lift your knees, keeping your feet flat on the floor. Arch your neck slightly, as if to look at the top of the wall behind you. Spread your arms out from your sides, just slightly apart from your torso. Lift one hand, with your elbow remaining on the ground. If your hand starts getting heavy, simply change hands.

PROCEDURE

Step One … Relax Your Physical Body:

Close your eyes and visualize something RED from nature … perhaps, an apple or a rose. Use this color as a mental trigger device to relax your physical body. While keeping the color red in your mind's eye, relax every muscle in your body. Start from the top of your head and finish with your feet. Imagine yourself with no muscles or joints.

Step Two … Release Your Emotions:

Visualize something ORANGE from nature ... perhaps an orange or a flower. This color is the mental trigger device to release and let go of negativity. While keeping the color orange in your mind's eye, feel yourself getting lighter as you "watch" negative emotions such as resentment flow away.

Step Three … Calm Your Mind:

Visualize something YELLOW from nature ... such as a banana or a flower. Use this color as a mental trigger device to calm and still your mind. While visualizing the color yellow, slow your mind down. Clear your mind of all negative thoughts, and watch them float away like yellow clouds.

Step Four … Sense Inner Peace:

Next, visualize something GREEN from nature ... perhaps a lawn or a tree. Use this color as a mental trigger device to sense inner peace. Allow yourself to experience an indwelling presence of peace and serenity.

Step Five … Feel Love:

Then visualize something BLUE from nature ... perhaps the sky. This color is the mental trigger device for feeling the emotion of love. As you visualize the color blue in your mind's eye, feel love radiating to you and through you to others ... as if you are a living conduit of love.

Step Six … Seek Wisdom:

Visualize something PURPLE from nature ... the deep indigo color of an eggplant or grapes. This color is the mental trigger device for aspiration. While keeping the color purple in your mind's eye, seek out the place within yourself and listen for insights regarding your gifts and true purpose.

Step Seven … Be Centered:

Finally, visualize something VIOLET from nature, such as orchids or tiny violets. Use this color as the mental trigger device for being centered. Accept that all people have gifts, value, and purpose … regardless of whether they realize it or not. Just experience whatever you are led to experience. Allow yourself to be still and quiet for several minutes.

Step Eight … Ending:

Repeat the following affirmation, *"Each day, in every way, I am getting better and better and better."* Then, slowly visualize the seven colors in reverse sequence. Starting with the inner most color violet and then moving up and out to purple. Next blue, then green … then yellow, orange, and red.
As you open your eyes, repeat the following, *"I open my eyes and I am wide awake. I am revitalized, refreshed, and in tune with life. I am enlightened. I am enriched. I am enthused. I am energized. I am. I just am."*

"The intuitive mind is a sacred gift
and the rational mind is a faithful servant.
We have created a society that honors the servant
and has forgotten the gift."
... Albert Einstein

"Chance favors the prepared mind"
... Louis Pasteur

"Look before you leap"
... Samuel Butler

"When your stomach disputes you,
lie down and pacify it with cool thoughts
... Satchel Paige

BOTTOM LINE

When overwhelmed, instead of getting hyper,
take the time to Center and get clear on your priorities.

EVALUATION

Acceptance Not Judgment

FIGHT

EMPATHY

People don't care how much you know …
until they know how much you care.

Chapter 6

Empathy – The Alternative to the Fight Reaction

If you really want to know what someone honestly thinks of you, just make them angry. Anger typically triggers truthful but negative comments such as, *"You are a liar;" "Do it this way, or you're fired;" "Your problem is you only think of yourself;" "I can't trust you,"* or *"I'm tired of your excuses."*

Conversely, when you are angry and demonstrating the Fight reaction by telling someone off or putting them down, the feelings and needs of your target are not your primary concern … you just want to tell the truth. Unfortunately, your Fight reaction provides justification for Fight, Flight, Freeze, or Facade in return, and thus the Reactive Cycle begins or escalates.

> *"Never get angry. Never make a threat. Reason with people."*
>
> … Don Corleone, The Godfather

It is easy to see how resistance and resentment are typical responses to the Fight reaction. Nobody likes to be yelled at, bullied, or pushed around, even when their own reactive behavior may have triggered an angry reaction in turn. No matter how justified your outrage, people will tend to react badly to you when they see you as angry or judgmental. The Fight reaction practically guarantees you will be attacked, ignored, lied to, or abandoned.

Stopping this reaction is difficult, as you must have perceived your Fight reactions as valuable to develop them in the first place. Perhaps, getting mad stopped people from picking on you. Arrogance may have helped you to bury hurt when a relationship did not work out. Possibly, you were admired for being tough. Maybe you learned and now believe that "nice guys finish last."

However strong it appears now, the Fight reaction is still *Fear-Based*. Other people trigger your negative behaviors. If they treat you right, you do not attack. If they do not treat you right, you attack. The bottom line is you are at the mercy of how other people treat you. You are not in charge of yourself when you demonstrate the Fight reaction.

Since the extreme Fight reaction is to become paranoid, the choice to come from Empathy seems pointless, foolhardy, or even dangerous. This is difficult to argue with, because the Fight reaction has one purpose … to protect you.

Whether you remember it or not, you would not be using the Fight reaction unless you were hurt while attempting to give or show love. When you showed kindness, you might have been laughed at. There may have been a time you tried to give love, but were rejected. Perhaps you were creative, but were criticized. Maybe you needed someone who abandoned you. Regardless, you eventually felt a need to protect yourself, and anger made you feel strong.

If you have ever uttered the phrase, *"If I've told you once, I've told you a thousand times"* you know how ineffective the Fight reaction truly is. Otherwise, your point would have been made once and for all the first time you shouted it.

The answer, when you are engaged in the Fight reaction, is to say exactly what you were going to snarl or shout, but do so with kindness and respect. Simply change HOW you say it, by adding Empathy.

> If what you are trying to communicate is important,
> say it in a way in which the intended receiver will hear it.

Empathy

To lack empathy, is to deny your own need for others. Abraham Maslow, in his famous 'Hierarchy of Needs,' defined one of the key motivators of human behavior as the 'belonging need,' or the need for people. This need can be filled by friendships, marriages, co-workers, religious acquaintances, comrades in arms, teammates, siblings, and anyone having similar interests.

All relationships have problems. With empathy, you do not start with the premise that the other person is an idiot just because you do not understand them. To do that is to guarantee your attempts to reach them, much less help them, will fail. You will not lead, as your reactions will be counter-productive to your aims and desires.

Empathy

The ability to relate to the feelings, emotions, thoughts, actions, and circumstances of others.

With empathy, even when you cannot comprehend why someone is behaving in a destructive manner … you understand that it somehow makes sense to them.

Many confuse empathy with sympathy, but they are very different. Just as with a sympathetic toothache, when the pain from one tooth feels like it is also coming from another tooth, a sympathetic person actually feels the pain of another. For example, a friend loses a job and is resenting his or her manager, so you resent the boss as well. If you feel bad, I feel bad. *"I can't understand why your boss fired you. He is such an idiot."*

With empathy, on the other hand, you understand how another feels, but it does not make you feel the same way. *"I understand you hate your boss, but resenting him is eating you up inside."*

Finally, a person with empathy does not take advantage of, ignore, or attack other people. He or she realizes there will be a consequence to such *Fear-Based* reactions. Because they can relate with others, they know how it would feel, and how they would react under similar circumstances. Valuable people may depart, and dangerous ones could mount a counter-attack. Either way, a price will be paid.

"There is no free lunch."

… Milton Freedman

The New Car Dealer

Tom was the owner of one of the largest car dealerships in the city. But, he had a problem. Tom had a good location, superb mechanics, excellent salespeople, but an inconsistent body shop. He finally found a small operation nearby, with an owner-operator who did impeccable work. However, it was not under his direct control. As a hands-on manager, Tom wanted to have the body work done in-house.

Finally, after several years resisting Tom's offers to work for him, the body shop man relented, and agreed to work for the dealership. It was a classic win-win agreement: Tom got an employee he could be proud of; his new employee got a state-of-the-art facility, and was given a free hand to run it as he saw fit.

Shortly afterwards, Tom's best friend had an accident with his new car. He needed it repaired for his anniversary the following weekend. He assured his friend that not only would the car be ready, but his new employee would make it look like new.

Three days later, the car was not finished. In fact, the repairs had not even been started. His new employee had been too busy setting up his new shop. Tom's normal reaction would have been to turn tyrannical and perhaps even fire the man … and all the effort he put in to hiring this worker would be lost.

Tom knew that if he gave in to his Fight reaction, his employee might simply quit and return to self-employment. Tom had to find another way to approach the problem.

Tom shifted to Empathy. He had already told his employee *"what"* he needed; now he had to tell him *"why."* Tom decided to take some time to sit down with his new employee and get to know him better. They spent time discussing the arrangements. Tom asked his employee how he felt about his new workshop, taking the time to really listen to his excitement and concerns. Eventually Tom asked, *"If you were me, and had to go tell a friend his car would not be ready for his anniversary, after you had promised him it would be ready, how would it make you feel?"*

Tom could see his new employee's eyes light up in understanding. He nodded, wished the man a pleasant afternoon, and then left him alone. No threats, no grilling, and no ultimatums. Unbeknown to Tom, the man immediately set to work to fix the car, going above and beyond the call of duty, pulling several late-night shifts to make sure the work was done on time. By painting an emotional picture that was easy to understand, he was able to relate his needs to his employee. The car was finished with time to spare, and the relationship, so close to a bad start, was firmly established with mutual respect.

> *"For to win one hundred victories in one hundred battles, is not the acme of skill.*
>
> *To subdue the enemy without fighting is the acme of skill."*
>
> … Sun Tzu

This story illustrates how, when you are about to employ the FIGHT reaction, you can come from the Empathy characteristic instead. Instead of turning dictatorial, appeal to the "feelings" of others. Take the time to re-state your purpose and commitments, especially when it seems they should be obvious to others. This is most important to do when you do not have the time…

Make The Time

The Problem … Your "FIGHT" Reaction

When demonstrating Fight reactions, you give ultimatums, become sarcastic, or attack. Whether you are actively seeking to fix something, finish something, or to punish someone, you say exactly what you mean. You are, or appear to be, unconcerned about the needs and feelings of others.

You will hear yourself asking **"What"** types of questions …
*"**What's** your problem?" … "**What** are you going to do about it?"*

When You Are Consumed With RESULTS, **Your Primary Characteristic Tends to Be JUDGMENTAL**

"I don't get mad, I get even."
"If you want something done right, you've got to do it yourself."
"The end justifies the means,"

Other Characteristics:

Aggressive	Manipulative	Arrogant	Sarcastic	Critical
Demanding	Intimidating	Insensitive	Offensive	Argumentative

The extreme Fight reaction is to become PARANOID

The Solution … Add EMPATHY

Avoid judgment and telling people WHAT to do. Look for something you can approve of or acknowledge. Take the time to explain WHY to others, or to ask WHY type questions. You need to forgive, give others courtesy, and let people give to you. Remember, it isn't what you say; it's how you say it.

> *"Tenderness and kindness are not signs of weakness and despair, but manifestations of strength and resolutions."*
>
> … Kahlil Gibran "The Prophet"

Balance Yourself by Focusing on …

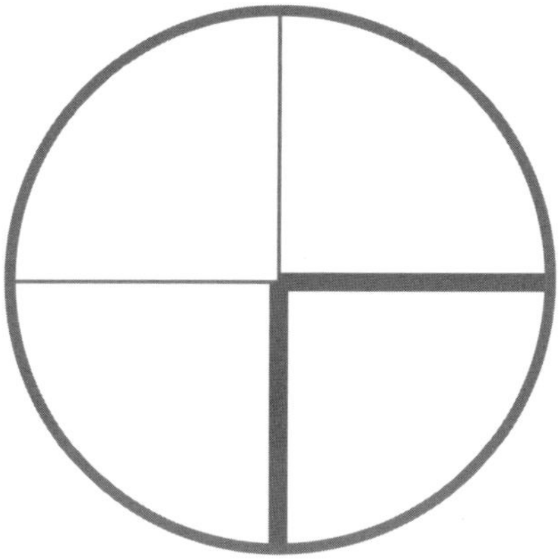

Choose to become …

Courteous	Supportive	Cooperative	Responsive	Kind
Friendly	Accommodating	Nurturing	Compassionate	Accepting

Focus on EMOTIONS and FEELINGS

The Tool: The Trust Formula

The core of the *Four E's of Excellence* is the ability to inspire trust, and thus gain support from others. In relationships, people who trust you will tend to listen to you, open up to you, date you, befriend you, endorse you, and want to be with you. In business, they will buy from you, hire you, promote you, and want you on their team. In politics, people who trust you will volunteer time, give you their vote, spread your message, and send you money.

There is a formula which can make gaining trust much easier. Consistent use of this formula has enabled many of my students to reach previously unreachable people. Of course, nothing guarantees how others will respond, but the "Trust Formula" will definitely increase your odds of a positive response.

When you demonstrate a *Fear-Based* reaction to others, you actually give them an excuse to react to you. Eventually, they will grow to expect your negative behavior and pre-act to you. The excellent leader strives to remove these excuses, by refusing to react in the first place. Here is an effective way to stay in control of yourself. When you are about to react, or pre-act, or demonstrate any programmed negative behavior, simply stop and think the following sentence ...

> *I honor you and I accept you,*
> *even though I don't understand you..*

When you are feeling angry and judgmental, and are about to attack, just stop for a moment and *THINK* this sentence. This pause will give you a chance to re-establish self-control, and choose an Empathetic alternative to a Fight *Fear-Based* reaction. It opens the door for forgiveness.

Unfortunately, the loss of self-control is all too common. If you are like me, you may have even reacted negatively when you first read this formula (see how easy it is to get you to react?). I actually laughed when I first heard it. I thought, *"If you do this formula when people are treating you wrong, they will eat you alive. You have opened the door to continued abuse."*

A typical reaction is to resist using the Trust Formula, even in a *"spilt milk"* Level-1 negative circumstance that happens at work or at home. Acceptance and honor are even more difficult to express following a Level-2 negative circumstance such as a firing, car accident, or crime. Forgiveness seems to be the rarest of commodities when there is a Level-3 negative circumstance … a death caused by alcohol, drugs, physical abuse, medical malpractice, murder, war, or a terrorist attack.

Nonetheless, this formula will help you to create trust … and give you a side benefit of reduced stress. You do not have to believe it. You do not have to like it. You do not even have to feel it. Just try it. What do you have to lose?

Other than exceptional leaders such as Jesus Christ, Mahatma Gandhi, Mother Teresa, and Martin Luther King, Jr., we do not tend to see the Trust Formula used in response to <u>any</u> kind of negative circumstance. When something goes wrong, what we see looks more like the following:

<u>Formula "B"</u>

I don't understand you.
Therefore, I don't honor you and I don't accept you.

How much of that kind of attitude do you see on a daily basis over "little" Level-1 negative circumstances at home, on the freeway, at work, in restaurants, in stores, and even in places of worship? The question is not, *"Does the Trust Formula work?"* The question should be, *"Is Formula B working?"* What is the predominance of Fight *Fear-Based* reactions doing to our children, our families, and our business relationships?

Using the Trust Formula

Here are some examples of how the Trust Formula can be used to effectively get you what you really want. When you have been taken advantage of in business, before you react, just stop and think the following ... *"I honor you and I accept you, even though I don't understand you."* When your spouse pushes your buttons, and you are about to counter-attack, bite your lip and say to yourself, *"I honor you and I accept you, even though I don't understand you."* When your son or daughter frustrates you with an obvious lie, before you explode just think, *"I honor you and I accept you, even though I don't understand you."* When you encounter challenging or negative clients, co-workers, employees, or employers in the workplace, just think, *"I honor you and I accept you, even though I don't understand you."*

Whenever something negative occurs and you are strongly tempted to employ a Fight reaction, use the Trust Formula, *"I honor you and I accept you, especially when I don't understand you."* Most people have to practice this many times before they see results. Nevertheless, they always see results, usually more quickly and profoundly than they expect.

The Trust Formula is designed to help you to gain self-control, not as a tool to control others. It is self-control, which demonstrates to others that you can be trusted.

An important safety tip: **Never speak the Trust Formula out loud.** It has a strange effect on a spouse or a boss when, in the middle of an argument you say, *"I honor you, and I accept you, even though I don't understand you."* It comes across as self-righteous and patronizing, and can make things worse.

Using the Trust Formula on Yourself

When you turn the Trust Formula inward, it has a wonderful effect on self-worth. Whenever you react to someone and start to regret your actions, instead of thinking, *"I should not have said that,"* simply say to yourself …

> *"I honor myself and I accept myself,*
> *even though I don't understand myself."*

We go through life trying to figure everyone else out. Yet how many of us truly understand ourselves?

Forgiveness

It could be said that to forgive is 'to give forth love' when you have been hurt. However, it does not mean that you condone the actions of the person you are forgiving.

Most people do not easily forgive when they have been hurt. Resentment makes it difficult. We feel justified in thinking, *"If I forgive you for what you did, it means your actions didn't matter and it lets you off the hook. Since they did matter, I will not forgive you."*

Whether it is by Fight, Flight, Freeze, or Facade, to resist forgiving is to rationalize the withholding of your love, abilities, and gifts. When you fail to forgive, you may or may not hurt the other person … but you definitely damage yourself.

> Behold the magnificent apple tree, which never says …
> *"I only give my apples to the deserving."*
>
> An apple tree which stops bearing fruit is dying,
> just as a human who stops giving love is dying.
> We die emotionally at first,
> but eventually the rest of the body follows.

Obviously, the person you are resenting benefits when you forgive. More significantly, however, you benefit when you forgive. Clearly the person who hurt you did not create the forgiveness … you created it. As such, to forgive another is to stay in charge of self. Such self-control is fundamental for the creation and maintenance of your self-worth.

Even when justified, negative reactions are still *Fear-Based.* It does not matter if your reasons are significant or shallow. The fact you can rationalize the behavior only proves you would not have acted in such a manner without a trigger. In other words, when you react, you are not the one in control.

Instead of reacting to your hurt, the answer is to use the *Four E's of Excellence.* Strive to find solutions to negative circumstances. Choosing to forgive when the conditions are hurtful, especially when you are tempted to react with hate, is a sign of excellence through self-control.

EXERCISE

In a normal day, you probably will not have any Level-3 or Level-2 negative circumstances (death or destruction). You will, however, have many Level-1 inconveniences. Face it, if you cannot control yourself when something small goes wrong, it is unlikely you will spontaneously develop into a great leader when big things go wrong. Practice on the small stuff.

1) Over the next 24 hours, practice the Trust Formula every chance you get. Keep track of each encounter. If someone cuts you off on the freeway, steals your briefcase, serves you the wrong food, spills milk, or laughs at you, pause and use the Trust Formula. Afterward, go ahead and react if you are still so inclined. Just get used to pausing before you do so.

Do this at least 5 times. Journal your insights:

____

____

____

____

____

2) Every time you react and forget to pause and think the Trust Formula, then turn it around and use the Trust Formula on yourself.

Do this at least 5 times. Journal your insights:

____

____

____

____

____

"We have been created to love and be loved"
… Mother Teresa

"Do unto others, as you would have them do unto you."
… Jesus, Matthew 7:12

"*The greatest thing you'll ever learn is*
just to love and be loved in return"
… Moulin Rouge

BOTTOM LINE

When coming from judgment of others,
employ the Trust Formula before acting...

"I honor you and I accept you,
even though I don't understand you."

When coming from judgment of yourself,
employ the Trust Formula afterward …

"I honor myself and I accept myself,
even though I don't understand myself."

EMPATHY

Negative Circumstances Create Outward Pressures

If you are not moving towards the center,
you are moving to the extremes. Stay in The Target Zone

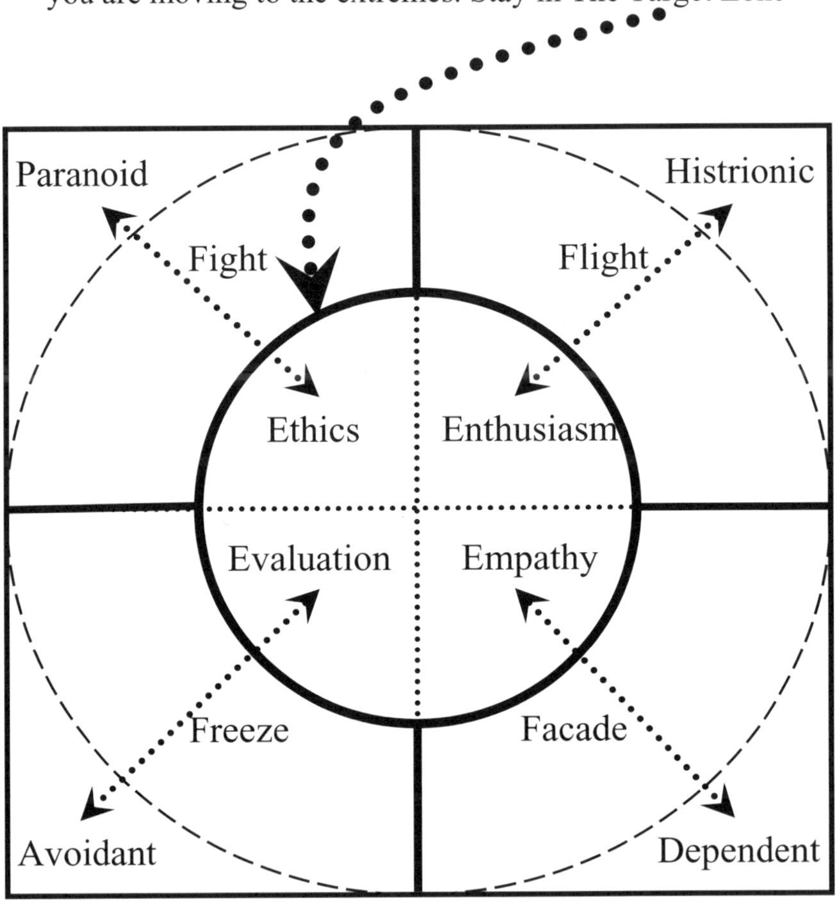

"Balance lives in the present … bring yourself back to the now."

… Oprah Winfrey

Chapter 7

Summary and Background of the Four E's

Each *Fear-Based* reaction is just one of the *Four E's of Excellence*, without its balancing opposite. Once you understand this, the solution becomes simple. When experiencing a *Fear Based* reaction, do not deny it or let it overwhelm you, simply ADD its balancing counterpart. Then, you remain in control of yourself.

BALANCE is the KEY

In essence, the Fight reaction is Ethics without Empathy,
so ADD Empathy

The Flight reaction is Enthusiasm without Evaluation,
so ADD Evaluation.

The Freeze reaction is Evaluation without Enthusiasm,
so ADD Enthusiasm

The Facade reaction is Empathy without Ethics,
so ADD Ethics.

Leadership excellence occurs when you overcome *Fear-Based* reactions, regardless of your circumstances. However, it is a "balancing" proposition. In times of stress or challenge, you will have a choice.

When experiencing a *Fear-Based* reaction, the choice is to either add Ethics, Enthusiasm, Evaluation, or Empathy (as the case requires), or to demonstrate Fight, Flight, Freeze, or Facade. This second "choice," when repeated enough, ceases to be a choice and places you in danger of losing self-control entirely … with one of the four Extreme *Fear-Based* reactions (Paranoid, Histrionic, Avoidant, or Dependent).

Choose Wisely

EXERCISE

Review the following four lists of attitudes, qualities, attributes, and behaviors. Circle (O) each one you feel you possess. Star (*) those which you have been able to demonstrate when stressed. The challenge here is to be honest with yourself.

Characteristics of Leadership Excellence

List A	**List B**	**List C**	**List D**
Accountable	Creative	Deliberate	Accepting
Bold	Energetic	Detailed	Accommodating
Confident	Enthusiastic	Diligent	Compassionate
Congruent	Exciting	Evaluative	Cooperative
Decisive	Expressive	Industrious	Courteous
Determined	Open	Integral	Empathetic
Ethical	Persuasive	Methodical	Friendly
Efficient	Positive	Patient	Kind
Focused	Promoting	Persistent	Nurturing
Honest	Spontaneous	Precise	Responsive
Thorough	Stimulating	Reliable	Supportive

Total the number of circled and starred items in each column:

____	____	____	____	____	____	____	____
O	*	O	*	O	*	O	*

The column with the most stars and circles is your strongest category. However, if your column with the most stars is not the same as the one with the most circles, you are probably not coming from your strengths in times of great stress.

Rank your own tendencies to demonstrate each of them. Use the results from this exercise, as well as insights from reading the previous descriptions of the *Four E's of Excellence …*

Ethics Enthusiasm Evaluation Empathy

Your primary quality: ______________________________
(pick one)

Your second most common quality: ______________________________
(pick a different one)

Your third most common quality: ______________________________
(pick a third one)

Your least demonstrated quality: ______________________________
(the last one)

<u>Hints:</u>

If you always say what you mean and it's, *"Damn the torpedoes, full speed ahead"** when faced with difficulties or challenges, your primary quality is probably ETHICS, and your least demonstrated is most likely EMPATHY … and you are certain of this. (*Admiral Farragut, 1864)

If you feel that you demonstrate all four qualities equally, your primary quality is probably ENTHUSIASM, and your least demonstrated is most likely EVALUATION. You will resist this, but you need to look deeper.

If you analyze this for more than a minute, and/or do not feel you are very strong at any of them, your primary quality is probably EVALUATION, and your least demonstrated is most likely ENTHUSIASM.

If you worry about what others might think of your choices, your primary quality is probably EMPATHY (you are pretty sure of this), but your least demonstrated is most likely ETHICS (which you almost certainly will deny, but you probably will admit to telling "white-lies").

Stay in the Target Zone

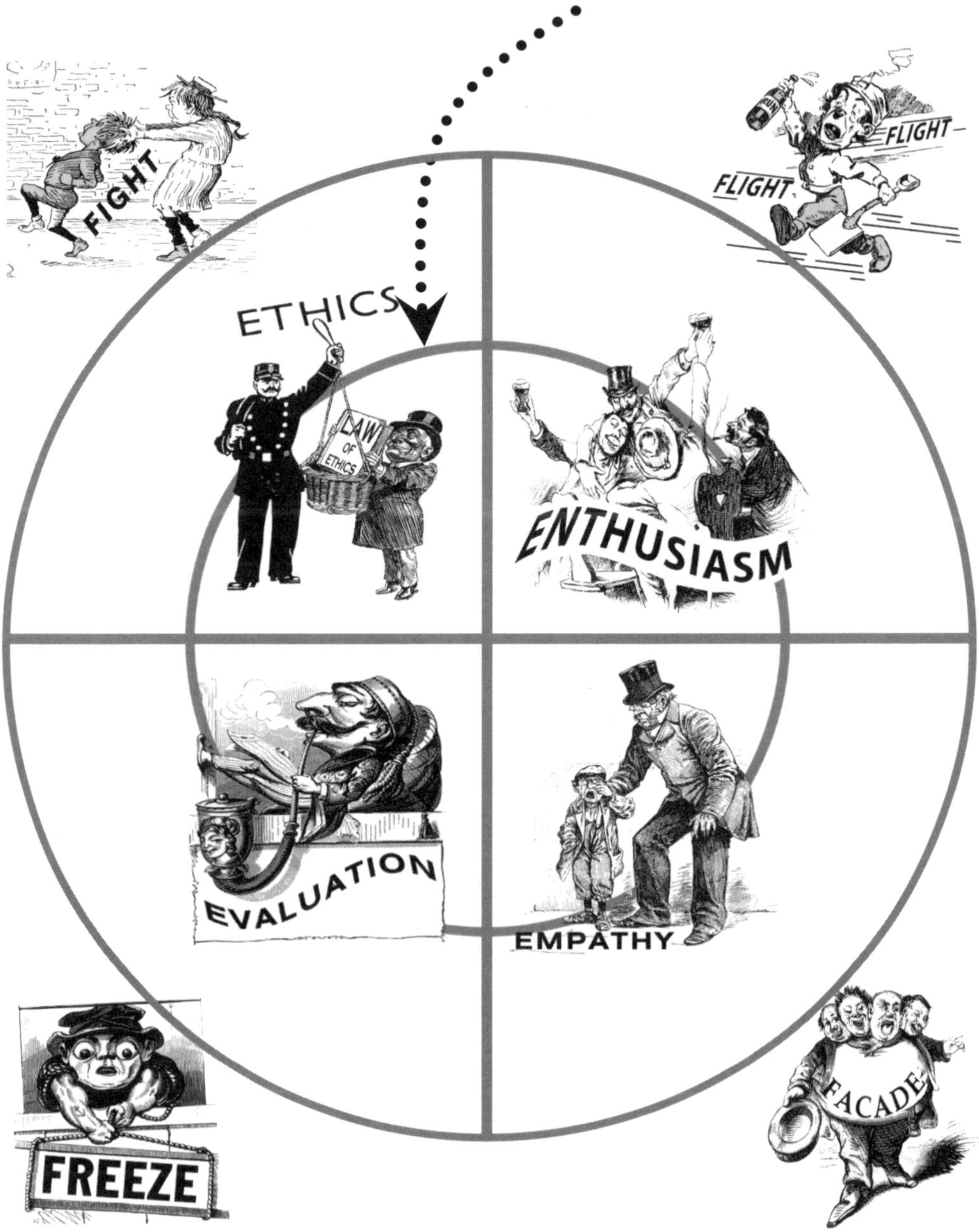

Summary – Using the Four E's

You are in …	**Fight**	**Flight**	**Freeze**	**Facade**
When you are negatively consumed with:	Results	Relationships & Time	Tasks and Commitments	Emotions & Feelings
Too focused on:	What?	Who/When?	How?	Why?
You are, or appear to be:	Aggressive Arrogant Critical Demanding Sarcastic	Distracted Harried Hurried Hyperactive Scattered	Anxious Inward Isolated Serious Withdrawn	Defensive Insecure Intimidated Phony Subordinate
Justified because you have become:	Judgmental	Frantic	Overwhelmed	Worried
You are at risk of becoming:	Paranoid	Histrionic	Avoidant	Dependent
	↓	↓	↓	↓
The Solution is to ADD …	**Empathy**	**Evaluation**	**Enthusiasm**	**Ethics**
Focus on:	Emotions & Feelings	Tasks and Commitments	Time for Relationships	Results
Tell others:	Why	How	Who & When	What
Become:	Accepting Compassionate Kind Nurturing Responsive	Deliberate Diligent Integral Patient Reliable	Creative Expressive Open Positive Promoting	Accountable Congruent Decisive Honest Thorough
Tool to Use:	Trust Formula	Centering	Planned Spontaneity	'Desired Results'
You Need to:	Forgive	Slow Down	Play	Risk
Give Others:	Courtesy	Information	Attention	Assurances
Let Others …	**Give to You**	**Help You**	**"In"**	**Know**

In about 400 BC, Hippocrates determined that human health and behaviors were influenced by the physical symptoms of blood, phlegm, and bile.
His "Four Temperaments" of people were …
Choleric, Sanguine, Phlegmatic, and Melancholic.

Galen, in about 150 AD, built upon the work of Hippocrates with his "Four Humors" …
Quick Tempered, Buoyant, Sluggish, and Dejected.

His was a system to cure disease based on a therapy of opposites (sound familiar?)

"Four Personality Styles" Behavioral Theory

Throughout history, there have been countless behavioral theories. They have come from religious, astrological, philosophical, psychological, psychiatric, and educational arenas. From Aristotle to Dr. Phil McGraw, there have been many people who have spent their lifetimes on quests for answers.

One of the oldest concepts of behavioral theory is, as I call it, the "Four Personality Styles." It first appeared as the astrological elements of Fire, Air, Earth, and Water. Then Hippocrates, Galen, and a few others until...

> In 1921, Dr. Carl Jung divided people into four personality "Archetypes"... Sensor, Intuitor, Thinker, and Feeler.

Building on his work, dozens of contemporary models have separated people into these same four groupings. Examples include Myers-Briggs, Ned Hermann's Brain Dominance Instrument, D.I.S.C., B.E.S.T., and Wilson Learning. Variations have appeared in *The 7 Habits of Highly Effective People, The Celestine Prophesy*, and even *Harry Potter*.

Two Benefits and Two Problems

Four-Style Personality Systems generally advance only one of two potential benefits. Some promote an increased personal effectiveness by learning one's own "Style" while many teach how to categorize the "Styles" of others.

1) Learning Your Own "Style"

The stated benefit of learning your personality style is; you are able to build on your strengths, while at the same time increasing your ability to predict your own negative behaviors. With this information, you will be able to make more effective choices.

While this is true, there can be a negative side effect to these systems. Instead of changing, people have been known to use this information to justify their own negative, non-productive, and destructive behaviors. I have heard comments such as, *"It's my personality style to be direct. It's your problem if you can't handle it."*

The Turtle and the Scorpion

Once upon a time a scorpion asked a turtle to give him a ride across a stream. The turtle refused saying, *"I'll get you to the middle of the stream and you will sting me and I'll die."*

The scorpion replied, *"First, you have to realize there is no way I'd sting you. If I killed you, then I would surely drown. Second, someday you might need a powerful friend and I would owe you one."* This made sense to the turtle. He always believed it was better to make a friend than an enemy, so he decided to give the scorpion a ride.

The scorpion climbed on the back of the turtle's shell and they entered the water. Everything went fine until the turtle felt a pain on his neck. Sure enough, the scorpion had stung him.

The turtle became paralyzed, but he managed to ask the drowning scorpion why he had stung him. The scorpion replied, *"I couldn't help myself. It's my nature."*

2) Categorizing the "Styles" of Other People

The benefits from these systems have been proven by organizations the world over. When armed with the knowledge of the four personality or behavioral styles, an owner, manager, or personnel department can more easily predict the likelihood of successfully filling a job opening.

When a prospective employer is striving to fill a position from equally qualified applicants, the job will go to the person with the appropriate "style" for the position. For example, an "Analyzer" accountant, a "Promoter" sales manager, a "Supporter" personnel manager, or a "Controller" plant manager (the "terms" are from the Integro-Persona Matrix system).

In the short term, there are definite advantages to both the organization and to the new employee. The problem with this "benefit" appears when there is an opportunity for advancement. People are often overlooked for promotion to a position for which they are qualified, because they are not viewed as possessing the "appropriate" characteristics. As a result of the ongoing stereotyping people get cubby-holed. Management then spends time, money, and effort to hire and train someone from the outside. This costs the organization even more when it loses a valuable, but frustrated, employee.

The Unique Advantage of The *Four E's of Excellence*

By studying several different systems, including my own *"People Wheel,"* and the interactions of the participants, I have become aware of the advantages and disadvantages of all adaptations of the "Four Personality Styles" Behavioral Theory. More importantly, I have observed an important problem inherent to them all (except Galen's)...

> All people do behave according to their primary style ... most of the time.
>
> However, nobody acts the same way all of the time, especially when they feel threatened.

The unique *Four E's of Excellence* system is based upon your being aware of your own current reactions, and not on the normal behavior or personality style of either yourself or others. Effective leadership results from changing your behaviors when stressed, instead trying to control, manipulate, ignore, or pacify others.

Following are 66 models (including *Four E's of Excellence)* that are in some way reflective of, or based upon, on the "Four Personality Styles." While this is an extensive list, there are bound to be omissions. The purpose of showing them here is simply to show the widespread application of this theory, and to show the similarity that exists among the differing models. "Four Personality Style" behavior systems have become so commonplace, that the Dilbert comic strip has even done a parody of them.

Some systems focus on improving self-awareness, others on learning to categorize and understand others. Interestingly, only Galen's system of curing disease with a "therapy of opposites" is similar in usage to *Four E's of Excellence,* which shows people how to 'cure' *Fear-Based* reactions with their personal "therapy of opposites."

Regardless of the manner in which each system interprets or utilizes the theory, notice how the labels of the "Four Personality Styles" generally remain consistent and synonymous, and of the patterns which emerge. For ease of comparison only, they are grouped into 'Typical Orientations' ...

Results	Relationships & Time	Tasks	Feelings & Emotions

A Collection of "Four Personality Styles" Models

Typical Orientation	**Style 1** **Results**	**Style 2** **Relationships and Time**	**Style 3** **Tasks**	**Style 4** **Feelings and Emotions**
Empedocles Four Qualities	Hot	Dry	Cold	Wet
Hippocrates Four Temperaments	Choleric (Angry)	Sanguine (Cheerful)	Melancholic (Sad)	Phlegmatic (Neutral)
Astrology	Fire	Air	Earth	Water
Sun Bear Medicine Wheel	Fire Thunderbird-Clan	Air Butterfly-Clan	Earth Turtle-Clan	Water Frog-Clan
Galen's Four Body Humors	**Quick-Tempered**	**Buoyant**	**Sluggish**	**Dejected**
Kretschmer's Four Temperaments	Hyperesthetic	Hypomanic	Melancholic	Anesthetic
Dr. Carl Jung Archetypes	**Sensor**	**Intuitor**	**Thinker**	**Feeler**
Myers-Briggs	Sensates	Intuition	Thinkers	Feelers
Marston's Emotions of Normal People	**Dominance**	**Inducement**	**Steadiness**	**Compliance**
John Geier D.I.S.C.	Dominance	Influence	Steadiness	Compliance
McQuaig Inst. Selling Styles	Dominance	Sociability	Relaxation	Compliance
Performance Trainers	Dominant	Extrovert	Patient	Conformist
B.E.S.T.	**Bold**	**Expressive**	**Technical**	**Sympathetic**
Wilson Learning	Driver	Expressive	Analytic	Amiable
Merrill & Reid Personal Styles	Driver	Expressive	Analytical	Amiable
Don Hutson Social Styles	Driver	Expressive	Analytical	Amiable
Cathcart & Alessandra	Director	Socializer	Thinker	Relater

Integro Persona Matrix	**Controller**	**Promoter**	**Analyzer**	**Supporter**
James H Quinn P. E. P.	Controlling	Promoting	Analyzing	Supporting
Jard DeVille	Controller	Entertainer	Comprehender	Supporter
Stuart Atkins L.I.F.O.	Controlling-Taking	Adapting-Dealing	Conserving-Holding	Supporting-Giving
Michael Lovas About People	Commander	Expressive	Thinker	Nurturer
Ned Herman Brain Dominance Instrument	Organize	Strategize	Analyze	Personalize
Allan Pease Questions are the Answers	Key #4 – Get a Commitment	Key #3 – Press the Hot Button	Key #2 -- Find the Hot Button	Key #1 – Melt the Ice
Hersey & Blanchard	Telling	Selling	Delegating	Participating
Quinn Inc. People Wheel	Congruent	Persuade	Deliberate	Accommodate
Adler's 4 Mistaken Goals	**Power**	**Revenge**	**Service**	**Recognition**
Simpson Conflict Styles	Power	Integration	Denial	Suppression
Personal Strategies	Power	Recognition	Respect	Approval
Thomas-Kilmann Conflict Mode	Competing	Collaborating	Avoiding	Accommodate
J. Hall Conflict Management	Win-Lose	Lose-Leave	Yield-Lose	Synergistic
Rinaldi Four Stress Responses	Fight	Flight	Freeze	Submission
Rosenban & Seligman Personality Disorders	Paranoid	Histrionic	Avoidant	Dependent
Robert E. Lefton	Dominant-Hostile	Dominant-Warm	Submissive-Hostile	Submissive-Warm
Adickes 4 World Views	Dogmatic	Innovative	Agnostic	Traditional

Mark Victor Hansen One Minute Millionaire	**Owls**	**Hares**	**Turtles**	**Squirrels**
Gary Smalley 4 Personalities	Lion	Otter	Beaver	Golden Retriever
Edward Horrell More Than Words	Lion	Porpoise	Fox	Koala
Taylor Hartman The Color Code	**Red Power**	**Yellow Fun**	**White Peace**	**Blue Intimacy**
Don Lowry True Colors	Gold- Be Prepared	Orange- Seize the Day	Green- Knowledge	Blue- I Care
David Keirsey 4 Temperaments	Red Artisans	Yellow Guardians	Green Idealists	Blue Rationals
A. H. Maslow Levels of Organization	**Autocratic**	**Motivational**	**Custodial**	**Collegial**
United States Constitution	The President	The Legislature	The Courts	The People
Ohio St. U. Leadership Model	High- Structure Low- Consideration	Low- Structure High- Consideration	High- Structure Low- Consideration	Low- Structure High- Consideration
Brewer Wynne & Ainsworth Power Mgmt.	Active- Competitive	Persuasive- Interactive	Precise- Systematic	Willing- Steady
Blake-Mouton Managerial Grid	Impoverished Management	Country Club Management	Task Management	Team Management
Keith Golay Learning Types	Conceptual- Specific	Actual- Spontaneous	Actual- Routine	Conceptual- Global
A. Gregorc Thinking Styles	Abstract- Sequential	Concrete- Random	Concrete- Sequential	Abstract- Random
B. McCarthy About Learning	Common Sense	Dynamic	Analytic	Imaginative
Allan Fahden Four Attributes	Creator	Advancer	Refiner	Executor
High School Standards Achievement	Ideas & Things	People & Ideas	Data & Things	People & Data
Spanger - Four Human Values	Religious	Artistic	Economic	Theoretic
Herb Shephard Philosopher	Perspective	Tone	Autonomy	Connectedness
George Sheehan The Four Roles	Saint	Animal	Craftsman	Friend

Stephen Covey The7 Habits of Highly Effective People	**Values & Commitment** **Spiritual**	**Stress Reduction** **Physical**	**Reading & Visualizing** **Mental**	**Service & Empathy** **Emotional**
Alexander Everett Mind Dynamics	Spiritual	Physical	Mental	Emotional
James H Quinn LifeStream	Spiritual	Physical	Mental	Emotional
Connie Chandler Paths of Mastery	Spiritual	Physical	Intellectual	Emotional
J. Janes Introcosm – Core Self	Agency	Physical Unity	Self History	Emotions
Robert Needlman Bound by Birth Order	First Born	Youngest Child	Only Child	Middle Child
James Redfield **Celestine Prophesy**	**Intimidator**	**Interrogator**	**Aloof**	**Poor Me**
Angeles Arrien Four Fold Way	Visionary	Warrior	Teacher	Healer
Don Miguel Ruiz The Four Agreements	Be impeccable with your word	Don't take anything seriously	Don't make assumptions	Always do your best
Ravi Batra The Great Depression Of 1990	Acquisitors	Warriors	Intellectuals	Laborers
The Four *Fear-Based* Reactions	**Fight**	**Flight**	**Freeze**	**Facade**
Four E's of Excellence	**Ethics**	**Enthusiasm**	**Evaluation**	**Empathy**
Just For Fun				
Harry Potter	Slytherin	Gryffindor	Ravenclaw	Hufflepuff
Bonanza	Ben	Little Joe	Adam	Hoss
Sex in the City	Miranda	Samantha	Charlotte	Carrie

Four E's of Excellence

PART THREE

Four E's of Excellence In Action

The vast majority of the world's largest
corporations in 1900 are no longer in business.

The Fortune 500 list from just 20 years ago,
only slightly resembles today's list.

The world is changing.
Current and past achievements do not
equate with future success.

Chapter 8
Leadership by Consensus

Over the last century, the premise in the business world has often reflected two principles. 1) The leaders of a company must have a clear vision and a strategic plan for its achievement. 2) Management's job is the successful implementation of that plan through the coordination of the skills and talents of employees and vendors.

However, despite the overwhelming emphasis on this traditional corporate *Position-Power* structure, many people today are operating out of alignment with corporate strategic plans. There is an increasing problem with staff turnover and employee dissatisfaction. More and more top-level employees are leaving to start their own businesses. Globalization, the Internet, and increasing political, social, and competitive pressures are having a dramatic effect upon the business culture in America, and everywhere else.

> The problem is the average employee has easy access to more knowledge and information than an entire corporation could obtain in the 1960's.
>
> As a result, they often have their own agenda of what is needed for the company.

When this occurs, it can place the employee out of alignment with corporate strategy, and reduce the effectiveness of even the best plans. *Position-Based* leadership is not typically open to independent thinking. Today, it is management's ability to create consensus with independent thinkers, which will determine the organization's ability to thrive.

Pro-Act

In the workplace, because almost everyone has his or her own agenda, people's needs, desires, and personalities often conflict. It might be nice to think of having a magic wand you could wave over everyone to bring instant harmony and accord, but the reality is that there will occasionally be adversity in even the best of families and corporations. However, your *Fear-Based* reactive efforts to take responsibility for changing anyone else's negative, non-productive, or destructive behaviors … are likely to be just about as effective as their attempts would be to change yours. Resistance, resentment, and revenge are the only likely results.

People may be ignorant of their own shortcomings, but they are not stupid. They have their own reasons for their *"Fear-Based"* behaviors … and will not change them for your reasons.

No matter how justified they seem, "eye-for-an-eye" reactions, or "bury your head in the sand" solutions only set the stage for the Reactive Cycle … which cannot work in the end. The only sustainable answer is to identify and overcome your *Fear-Based* reactions with *The Four E's of Excellence.*

The alternative to reacting to a problem, or pre-acting to the possibility of a problem, is not necessarily easy to do. However, it is simple. You simply notice how you are reacting or pre-acting, and, then choose to do something different. Almost anything would be an improvement, but conscious decisions to implement the *Four E's of Excellence* will produce the most effective results.

Unfortunately, because we have been so thoroughly conditioned to be reactive, there is not even a word for the opposite of "react" in the dictionary. The closest you could find was "act," which implies a phony or artificial response. However, a word has been coined which does work. Instead of reacting, we can now choose to "Pro-Act."

> To Pro-Act is to become a professional at living.

Instead of a *"do as I say, not as I do"* approach, pro-acting is the demonstration of the alternatives you would choose to have others implement, regardless of negative circumstances or hurt feelings. Because effective leaders are pro-active, they tend to solve problems … and often prevent them from occurring in the first place.

Imagine that you are attacked while walking down the street to catch a bus to work. You are punched violently and knocked to the ground. Your attacker then jumps on your chest and strikes your face while swearing at you and spitting. It is painful, insulting, and disgusting. You have never seen this person before, and have no clue as to why this is happening. How would you react?

Depending on the size of the threat, your abilities, and your training, you might fight back or run away. Otherwise, if you could not get away, you could yell for help and cover-up to reduce the damage. You might even try to talk the person into stopping by telling him what you think he wants to hear. Fight, Flight, Freeze, or Facade. Because you are angry, frantic, confused, or scared, you would employ at least one *Fear-Based* reaction to protect yourself.

Now imagine a second scenario. You are walking down the street and hear the squealing of brakes. You turn and observe a car striking a pedestrian. He literally flies through the air and lands at your feet. Blood is spurting from his arm, where a bone is protruding.

You become pro-active as you bend down to help the man, but in his delirium, he strikes you harder than the previous attack. This man is also swearing and spitting as he continues to hit you. It is as painful as the first example, but with more swearing and saliva. Blood is ruining your clothing.

With even more negativity than the previous circumstance, how would you react? Would you react the same way as the first example? If you bent down to help the person and were hit, would you stand up, kick them, and leave in anger? Of course not. You would remain pro-active.

You might wrap the wound in your good shirt, even while blocking the punches. If a drunk offered to help, you would keep him away. If an ambulance showed up you would turn the victim over to them in a heartbeat. You would be determined, careful, and open for help. You would be an effective leader even while enduring pain, spit, fear, and insults. You would do so even if you had been depressed all morning.

There is only one difference between the two examples. In the second example, you could see *"why"* you were being hurt. Because of this you did not take the 'attacks' personally, and you were able to maintain self-control.

The Restaurant Manager

The following letter regards a serious business problem, and a solution. It is a true story of a breach of trust. Do not simply read the letter. Imagine yourself as each of the three people, and ask yourself how you would have reacted had you been in their place.

Read carefully, and read between the lines. You will see all four *Fear-Based* reactions … none of which actually manifested. If any of the three people involved had succumbed to their initial urges, it would have had a much different conclusion.

> Excellent leaders create leaders, not followers.

Dear Ross,

I want you to know that today you've made a difference in my brother's life, and he hasn't even met you. Here is what happened.

My brother owns a restaurant in Texas. Two weeks ago he discovered money was missing from a deposit. He asked the manager if he had any idea what happened to it. The manager said, *"I won't lie to you. I took it. I planned to pay it right back, but it's taken longer than I thought. I'm sorry."*

My brother's policy on this stuff is clear. You fire the guy, no matter what. We spoke on the phone the day it happened. I suggested to my brother a revolutionary concept. Instead of making a *Fear-Based* decision, I challenged him to find a creative "win-win" solution. I gave him an alternative to firing this man, but I got off the phone thinking my words had fallen onto deaf ears.

Two hours later my brother called back. He'd met with the manager. The man came to my brother's office with a check from his parents for the entire sum he took. His wife came with him.

My brother asked him why he took the money. He took it to pay for his daughter's doctor bill. He knew he was losing his job. He just wanted to make it right.

To make a long story short, my brother did not fire him. He put the man on probation, and demoted him to a position where he won't handle money, but will be able to earn a living. My brother then gave him part of the money he'd taken as an advance on his salary (since he knew things were tight).

My brother tells me that before I told him about acting out of love instead of fear, he would never have considered keeping this man on. It would not have mattered how loyal he'd been, or how compelling the circumstances.

From what I know about this situation, and how my brother dealt with it, I believe he took a potentially tragic episode and turned it into a wonderful opportunity. This man might well become the most loyal, devoted employee my brother will ever know, just because someone was willing to take a chance on him. For one moment my brother ran his company with wisdom and compassion, not fear. Even that one moment is a tremendous gift."

So, Ross, here is how you made the difference. First, I didn't even know the words "Fear-Based reacting" until you taught them to me. Second, I would never have suggested such a novel approach to anyone in my family (even if I knew it was the right thing), simply out of fear they would reject me. Because of that, my brother touched his manager.

That man has a job this Christmas because I had the courage to risk rejection for something important, and because my brother had the courage to think "outside the box." Who knows whom his manager will touch because of all of this?

As for me, I'm willing to keep risking for what I believe in. Thank you Ross for showing me that I could make a difference.

Merry Christmas,

Love (Name withheld by request)

"For one moment my brother ran his company with wisdom and compassion, not fear. Even that one moment is a tremendous gift."

I cannot win and sustain it …
… unless you also win.

You cannot win and sustain it …
… unless I also win.

The Win-Win Principle

Increasingly, successful organizations are defined by their ability to align human resources to achieve corporate objectives. The biggest business winners in the 21st Century will be corporations run by excellent leaders, who operate their companies in accordance with the "Win-Win" principle.

While this concept is well known, it seems poorly understood and often undervalued in the modern corporate culture. As an employer, you may think you are succeeding when you get more than you give to your employees. If you are a smart employer, you have hired smart employees. Such people know when they are being taken advantage of. Ultimately, they will react to you. You will lose your best people. They will either quit or hold back. Either way, you and your company stand to lose out.

As an employee, you might feel you are getting away with something by leaning on another person or working for more than you are really worth. At best, you will fail to achieve your potential. At worst, you could be overlooked for promotions or even fired.

By adhering to the "Win-Win" principle, excellent leaders rise to the top. As employees, these people give more than they expect in return. They arrive early and stay late. These people ask, *"What can I do to help take this company to the top?"* They become leaders by studying the industry and the competition, and freely share ideas that will improve their company.

In sales, excellent leaders make sure their customers get what they want, when they want it … and are continually looking for ways to provide added value. Commitments are completed earlier and better than expected, and the client always gets more than they paid for.

In management, these people take care of their employees. They do not play politics. They ethically reward and promote the effective employees who contribute the most. They know that their professional success depends on the success of every member of their team. Those who really desire to succeed will inspire their people to discover reasons to implement the *Four E's of Excellence*.

If you are working for an organization that does not follow this principle, you are not helpless. You have the same 3 choices as 'George' (Chapter 2)…

1) Change the company from the inside.
2) Get a job with a company that recognizes and rewards value.
3) Start your own company.

Consensus is the result of both
Individual Choice and Teamwork.
Getting there is the art of
leading a group to a single agreement...

*"This is the best alternative we all can,
and **will**, support … even if, individually,
we each feel there is a better choice."*

Creating Consensus

The effective leader strives to create consensus in order to achieve results through others. Egos must be put aside. Begin with the premise that there is seldom a single solution to any problem. Unanimity is rarely achievable, and is not the goal of consensus.

When there is consensus the people of the organization are in agreement, *"We have the best product, or president, or pricing"*, or *"We have to save our jobs"*, or *"We have to beat off-shore competition."* When the people of an organization are in consensus, their various tasks and activities automatically operate in alignment. This synergy is actually the by-product of consensus, and not a goal within itself.

Typically, when we spend time debating the best approach to solving a problem there are winners and losers. The winners may or may not be arrogant about their victories, but the losers are invariably resentful. The *Four E's of Excellence* in business is a roadmap for eliminating this resistance. The two objectives of consensus are:

1) Group alignment for the process of solving a problem.
2) Group celebration for each failure, as well as for success.

In my outdoor leadership seminars, I have noticed that groups have often spent more time debating the best solution to a problem-solving game, than it would have taken to test every single one of the suggestions. Further, once a solution was found, those who saw their ideas tossed aside usually did not celebrate the victory.

Fighting for your solution can cause others to resist your ideas and suggestions, and to resent you if their ideas are ignored. By endorsing other ideas before your own, effective alternatives are often found. Besides, it is usually better to have consensus on an 'inferior' solution than resistance on a 'perfect' one.

When striving to achieve consensus, there is a tendency for numerous small groups within an organizations to come to identical solutions to problems … with one exception. If the president, owner, or manager is in one of the groups, that group will typically reach a different conclusion.

The most likely reason is that many people loathe being rejected by a poor manager so they give input very carefully. Thus, ideas are lost. Conversely, in an effort to help excellent managers, people tend to filter their input in order to either make their boss's decisions easier, or to impress them. Again, ideas are lost. In both cases it is the *Position-Power* of the boss, real or presumed, which prevents true consensus.

Regardless of the reason, consensus requires the traditional boss/leader to be absent from the group problem-solving scenario. It also requires the boss/leader to implement the decision of the group. Otherwise, there is no point to the exercise.

> Whether they realize it or not, business and governmental leaders typically make their decisions without all of the facts.
>
> <u>Consensus is the only effective alternative.</u>
>
> The larger the number of people involved in a decision, the more perfect the answer becomes.

Guidelines for Creating Consensus

Making a decision, which only involves you, is difficult enough in life. Working together in a family, where individuals have different wants and needs can be frustrating, to say the least. However, opposition to the creation of consensus within an organization can be overwhelming. This is because most businesses are still run by dictatorial, *Position-Power* based management. Fortunately, when done properly, the creation of consensus is still possible in those companies.

Solving problems with consensus involves change, and the normal reaction to change is resistance. In order to overcome this resistance, all participants must commit to keep the following agreements.

#1: Advance Agreement to a Final Decision

For large organizations, form discussion groups of from 5 to 8 people. For small companies and families, one group is ample. The members of each group need to agree in advance to support the final decision of the group, even if they disagree with that decision.

#2: Agreement of Equality of Opinion

All people must be prepared to share their position as logically as possible, but each person agrees to avoid arguing for their own solution. Conflicts need to be avoided, but be wary of quick agreements which may mean that some ideas have been left unspoken. Always make sure everyone has shared at least one idea.

#3: Agreement to Seek Acceptable Alternatives

All members agree to seek out next-best acceptable alternatives when an impasse occurs, and that there will be no voting. Each person agrees to yield only to positions that have some logic, and at least a possibility of success, even if individually they feel there is a better solution.

The first step in achieving consensus within an organization,
is to break the organization into small groups.
Consensus, within each small group, occurs when
each person is able to say, about a specific idea or plan …
***"I agree that this is the best solution
we can all agree on,
and that it has at least some possibility of success,
and that I will support it …
even if I feel there is a better solution."***

Consensus, for the larger group or organization,
occurs when all groups come up with
the same or similar answer in this fashion.

However, when any number of small groups
come up with significantly different answers,
Consensus will only occur when all groups are able to say,
About one of the specific plans,

***"I agree that this is the best solution
we can all agree on,
and that it has at least some possibility of success,
and that I will support it …
even if I feel there is a better solution."***

The Distributor

A distributor of five products had a high quality line of stuffed animals. Most of its sales came from just one of these lines. Unfortunately, because the other four products had such low sales, the suppliers were threatening to change distributors. This would mean a potential loss of 25% of their total sales revenue, and would mean the company would not be able to cover its fixed costs.

The president knew he had to do something, so he started to demand increased sales from the other four product lines. He tried threats, contests, pleading, and bonuses. Nothing worked.

I was hired to conduct a "motivational" seminar for this company. I set out to discover what was motivating the sales force to focus only on one product, even when they knew they needed to sell the other four as well. The first thing that I discovered was a "Comfort Zone." By selling the stuffed animals, which required little effort, almost everyone on the sales force was making a good living.

The second thing I discovered was the contests, the boss's pleas, the bonuses, and the threats had little or no effect because of *Fear*. Almost to a person, the sales force was worried about losing existing customers. They thought it might upset their customers to push products that had already been refused. Additionally, it was felt that prospective customers would probably only be interested in the stuffed animals, so they did not want to blow new sales by pushing the "wrong" products.

This was interesting, but it did not give me what I was looking for. I sat down with the president to discuss my findings. He spoke to me of his desire for employees to be successful, and he reiterated his concern that they were not responding to his requests.

I discovered the company policy that had unintentionally set this up. The president told me he especially wanted new hires to be successful so efforts at training them would not be wasted. He encouraged his managers to help new hires create a customer base with the easier to sell stuffed animals.

I was impressed. This man was actively pursuing the win-win concept. The new hires would win by receiving commissions that exceeded their minimal training "draw." The managers would win with higher bonuses tied to their total sales volume. The president would win by increasing sales and reducing the amount of time he had to pay a training draw.

My second step was to conduct a problem-solving session with the managers, sales-people, and the president. First we broke into small teams to solve a hypothetical problem. Everyone learned the basics of how to create answers by "consensus."

Once they had the idea, I presented the boss's dilemma, *"How can we get the sales force to sell more of the four "other" products?"* Each team was to come up with a possible solution. The only ground rule was each team member had to be able to support the team's idea, even if they personally thought there was a better answer.

One by one, as I read the suggestions, I was shocked at their similarity. Interestingly, the only dissimilar idea came from the team that included the president. As I reviewed the ideas, the solution became obvious.

I made the following recommendation to the president: *"Because of your desire for new hires to be successful, everyone is consumed with selling stuffed animals. You need to change your training policy in order to affect a shift in thinking to increase your sales of the other four products."*

"Your new hires," I continued *"should only sell the other four products. They need to reach a certain sales volume with those products before they are ALLOWED to sell the stuffed animals. This will have two benefits. Your managers will become more proficient at training new hires to sell the four products, and your new hires will have customers who want those products."*

Then I told him, *"You already know a trained salesperson can sell the stuffed animals to existing customers. Therefore, the sales of a new hire will dramatically increase from the moment they get to add the stuffed animals to their product line. You might be out-of-pocket with their "draws" a bit longer, but your total sales volume should increase."*

After a meeting with his managers, the president decided to implement the new training policy. As far as I could tell, he really had nothing to lose.

A year later I was invited back to do a follow-up seminar. This is always a good sign. I asked about the results of my suggestion the previous year. The president smiled and told me, *"Sales of the four products are up 50% and growing. The best part is that stuffed animals sales are up 20% as well. Our suppliers are happy and we are even looking at adding a few new items. Things couldn't be better."*

I asked him to explain what he thought had happened to turn things around. The president said the minute his managers had to focus on the other four products in their training of new hires, everything changed. As I had guessed, when the new hires became proficient at selling the other four products, they had little trouble selling the stuffed animals. But, something else happened.

Probably due to the shift in focus by each sales manager, virtually all sales-people began selling more of the other four products. They also were selling more of the stuffed animals.

The president became a more effective leader when he began to realize his people did things for their reasons and not his. When he became flexible enough to change a favorite policy on the chance it was causing the problems he was plagued with, his people responded immediately. Effective solutions always reach someone, but in this case they benefited everyone.

Every time management fails to change
an undesired "collective" behavior
of its employees, it turns out that there is
a company policy which actually causes,
and even rewards, this behavior.

Discover and change the policy,
and you change the behavior.

It Always Works.

"Well Days" at the Warehouse

Another company's needs for an accurate and timely inventory traditionally caused great stress between Christmas and New Year's. This difficult task was compounded, as many employees tended to call in sick during this period. Threats, directives, pep talks, and staff meetings all failed to correct this situation, which was destroying morale and productivity. However, it was solved easily and quickly through consensus.

Near the end of a one-day seminar on consensus, I put this problem to the staff. First, they broke into small groups to solve a hypothetical problem. Then, each team was instructed to come to a consensus on what was causing this year-end rash of sick-days, and what their solution would be. As always, I insisted the president of the company be in one of the groups.

Virtually every consultation I have been involved with has had a similar conclusion, which held true to form for this company as well. All groups, except the president's, came up with the same reason for the problem, and the same solution.

The Cause: Company policy stated "sick days do not accumulate." Since sick days are lost if not used in any one calendar year, people who had not used theirs felt they would be cheated of paid time off, simply because they had stayed healthy. They viewed sick days as a perk, and therefore called in sick at the end of the year. Indeed, many people had even gotten to the point of planning for this eventuality so they would have extra time to prepare for the holiday season.

The Solution by Consensus

The company should change their policy to allow employees to use either paid "sick days" or "well days" … neither of which would accumulate.

The Result: People could call in "well" on a nice summer day, and not have to worry about getting caught. They could even show off their tans. Stress levels plummeted. Most people used up their "sick" or "well" days by the holidays. The few who chose to take well days at that time of the year were minimal. In fact, these people were not resented because everyone else knew they themselves had taken advantage of this policy during the year.

Courage

There is no trick to demonstrating the *Four E's of Excellence* when life is working. The challenge is to possess these leadership qualities when something, or everything, goes wrong. Whether you are threatened with losing something you want, or with getting something you do not want, courage is the one characteristic you will need to be able to control yourself, as opposed to losing control or trying to control those around you.

> *"What've they got that I ain't got?"*
> ... asked the Cowardly Lion.
>
> *"Courage."*
> ... replied Dorothy, the Scarecrow,
> and the Tin Man.

Yes, it can be challenging to identify and overcome our own *Fear-Based* reactions to any negative circumstance. However, to inspire others to do likewise is the true test of leadership. Your ability to discover and implement solutions requiring consensus, will be in direct proportion to your willingness to be courageous. Courage, however, is not the lack of fear. To have courage is to act when afraid.

When people observe others achieving personal and professional success, seemingly without fear, they often reach an erroneous conclusion. They think fear itself is the problem. Therefore, they decide, it will be by eliminating their fears that they will be similarly successful.

Effective leaders are sensitive to their fears. However, they are neither overwhelmed by their fears, nor are they in denial of them. They are able to make conscious decisions to sometimes risk <u>despite</u> fears, while at other times to be cautious <u>because</u> <u>of</u> fears.

While we seek out feelings of joy and happiness in our quest for success, it is fear that may actually be the most valuable feeling of all. Fear of being hurt can keep us alive when there is danger. Fear of loss can warn us when we should not trust someone. Fear of dying can give our lives a sense of urgency.

Rock climbing, for example, begins with the assumption something will go wrong. The high levels of fear to the real risk of falling, become only perceptions of risk with the proper use of safety equipment. It is not courageous to face danger without proper planning and clear agreements. It is foolhardy.

> Having fear is not the problem.
>
> Eliminating fear is not the solution.

My daughter, Kelcey, once overcame her fears to climb a 50-foot rock face. Her courage to overcome her fear of falling was inspirational. It was made possible because of quality safety equipment and expert supervision. Several times she fell, screamed, laughed about it, and continued climbing.

However, after completing her climb and unhooking her equipment, Kelcey jumped for joy off a small boulder and sprained her ankle. Because of her lack of fear, she perceived no need to plan for something going wrong. As a result, jumping off a little rock nearly caused a broken leg.

With jobs and relationships, just as with rock climbing, begin with the assumption things will go wrong. Pre-planning and clear agreements are the career and relationship equivalents of a climbing harness and properly manned safety ropes.

Rejection in business is always a possibility when you strive for consensus, ask for a sale, interview for a job, or make a presentation. However, just as falling while attached to a safety rope is not harmful, there is no real danger from rejection. You may not enjoy the feelings of rejection, but you are no worse off than before. Shake it off, learn from the experience, and do it differently the next time.

If you were to conduct a study of all effective leaders, you would find many differences. Nonetheless, at their core you would discover ONE common characteristic … courage. This element consistently separates the successful from the unsuccessful, and the great from the average.

Without fear, no act is courageous. Fear is required. Courage is an inspirational victory over fear. It empowers you to overcome *Fear-Based* behaviors such as insecurity, anger, anxiety, procrastination, worry, indifference, obsession, and denial.

Whenever you have a *Fear-Based* reaction to negativity, you give your personal power away. Until you stop giving your power away, you will always find a way to fail. The cure for this "disease" of negativity is courage. When you develop the courage to do those things you fear, you become the master of your own life.

The single greatest reason people fail to succeed is the destruction of their personal power. Regardless of whether your self-worth was destroyed as a child, or your self-esteem has been trashed as an adult, your personal power can be restored with courage. The only moment that matters is now.

> Leadership Excellence requires:
>
> 1) The wisdom to recognize and deal with "real" risks, regardless of LOW sensations of danger.
>
> 2) The courage to overcome "perceptions" of risk, regardless of HIGH sensations of danger.

EXERCISE

Take a current situation at home or at work. Organize a group session to create a solution using consensus. Test the idea and journal what happened.

____

____

____

____

____

____

____

<u>Suggestion</u>: Start small.

Four E's of Excellence

CHAPTER 9

Relationships and Giving

The business and educational segments of our society have done a remarkable job in the development and teaching of "job" skills. People are generally competent at their jobs. They know what to do and how to do it. Nevertheless, today we find many competent people are failing to excel or even to survive because they lack "relationship" skills. They do not know how to develop and maintain trusting relationships.

You have no doubt heard the lie, *"It takes two people to make a relationship work."* Actually, it does NOT take two people to make a relationship work, but it does take two people to destroy one.

The truth, it only takes ONE person to make a relationship work. Furthermore, you have always known this. You have just believed it was the 'other' one.

> Whenever there has been a problem in a relationship, invariably, you have both thought *"everything would be just fine,"* if only the 'other' ONE would change something.

A 'relationship' is a noun. It is just a thing. A relationship is simply a connection between people or groups who are dealing with each other. Everyone has relationships. We have relationships with spouses, friends, co-workers, and people at church. We have them with rebellious teenagers, uncooperative employees, ex-spouses, grumpy waiters, former employers, and problem clients. We even have a relationship with the other drivers on the highway, the rest of the audience in a play, and the small group of people who join us on a flight or an elevator ride. However brief, the existence of a relationship has nothing to do with its depth or quality, or your desire to maintain or improve it.

It is the ability to RELATE with others, which determines the effectiveness of our relationships. The word 'relate' is a verb. It is an action.

The dictionary definition is, *"to have a friendly or close relationship with another, or others … to be responsive or sympathetic."*

Stress is a normal result of personal, intimate, and business relationships. The common denominator in our lives is we must relate with people when there are problems and conflicts. So why is it we are usually able to relate with some people, but rarely with certain others? The answer is directly proportional to the existence of mutual trust.

> While we would prefer to relate with only the people we trust, situations often require us to relate with people when trust is lacking.

There is a quandary when you decide to trust another person. Regardless of the potential benefits, you are open to the possibility of being hurt. Conversely, when you do not trust, regardless of the hurt you may avoid, you guarantee lost opportunities for the achievement of desired results such as success, love, friendships, and self-worth.

It is easy to create an atmosphere in which you are not trusted. Simply break your word, show up late, gossip, judge, attack, lie, cheat, or violate confidences enough times and even profoundly valuable professional and personal relationships can be ruined. With some people, even one time is enough to break the trust permanently. Once gone, regaining trust is difficult and often impossible.

In both business and personal relationships, if you gain an "advantage" over others by abusing trust, there is always a cost. Not the least of which is a guarantee the advantage cannot be sustained. If your behavior threatens others, ultimately they will react to you in one of four ways. They will attack you, leave you, shut you out, or lie to you … or some combination thereof. Are any of these possible negative reactions truly in your best interest?

In business, ethics demand you keep your word to employers and clients. Regardless of the reasons, if your behavior causes others to lose trust in you, you lose.

Many people resist giving when they take a job. Instead of exceeding expectations, they give just enough to keep from getting fired. This is probably fair, since these types of people seem to end up working for bosses who only pay their employees just enough to keep them from quitting. Everyone is worried about what they are going to get, instead of concentrating on what they have to give. With so many adversarial working relationships, it is no wonder so many businesses are failing to thrive.

The same is true with personal relationships. Some people get married seeming to look for excuses to stop giving. They do not mean it when they say, *"I promise to love, honor, and cherish until death do us part."* What they might as well have said is, *"I promise to tolerate you until I feel like killing you."*

The ethical spouse keeps the promise, *"to love, honor, and cherish until death do us part,"* regardless of the issues and problems. He or she finds a way to enjoy their partner's little quirks. They maintain their integrity and honor their promise to cherish, no matter what it takes.

The ethical spouse cherishes Level-1 negative circumstances such as the toilet seat left up, or the make-up left all over the counter. If their spouse consistently leaves the cap off the toothpaste tube, instead of allowing a *Fear-Based* reaction, they make a conscious choice to keep their word and cherish the growing glob of toothpaste on their counter. Of course, they may also buy a second tube and hide it just out of arm's reach.

Once people begin to take it personally when something goes wrong, they begin to resent their partner for the smallest of challenges, and the Reactive Cycle begins. Once begun, it is difficult to stop. Mild *Fear-Based* reactions, such as arguing and sarcasm, accelerate toward affairs and abuse. When a marriage ends, there are always excuses and accusations. Usually, both people end up claiming the divorce was their spouse's fault. However, neither one ever seems to blame the real culprit … the *Fear-Based* reactions to little problems which led each partner to rationalize withholding love from each other in the first place.

> Most people would rather be right than happy.
> In fact, it is almost okay to be miserable,
> as long as you can prove it is not your fault.

Roberta and Me

I met Roberta Lee Rockefeller while at the University of Southern California. We were inseparable. We were lovers and best friends. Shortly after I graduated, we decided to get married. We lived in Los Angeles, and each had our own convertible sports car. We had good jobs, spent a lot of time at the beach, and had many friends. Not only were Roberta and I on "The Newlywed Game," we won. We really did have a great life together.

After three years of marriage, we decided to have children. Roberta gave birth to Kelcey, the first of our three daughters. Jancy and Carly followed two and four years later, respectively. I was the proud papa of three beautiful, healthy, intelligent girls.

We should have been the picture of joy. However, we were not happy. Roberta had wanted children since she was a child. Roberta's feelings for our daughters were more important than her need for my friendship. She did not ignore me after they were born; I simply stopped being her best friend. In retrospect, I do not think my ego ever allowed me to be anything other than Roberta's best friend.

I always had a fear of divorce. My parents had been married for decades, as had Roberta's. I actually had made the commitment to never do anything 'wrong.' If there were ever to be a divorce, it would not be my fault. Accordingly, I never had an affair, used drugs, or got drunk. There were no beatings, expensive hobbies, or gambling. I worked hard, earned a good living, and provided a nice home for my family. I never did anything wrong (I hope you can see what is coming).

Now, all relationships have problems. I, of course, never did anything wrong. Therefore, who had to be causing all the problems? Correct. Roberta.

Roberta was clearly the problem. Surely, you can see that? (It still amazes me that she was able to put up with this self-righteousness for 10 years. Obviously, she loved me a lot). So I became critical, offensive, and judgmental of practically everything Roberta did, or did not do. I may not have been happy, but it certainly was not my fault (I try to imagine what it must have been like living with me, but I really cannot).

Finally, she had enough. Ours was one of the first "no-fault" divorces in Illinois. It only cost a few hundred dollars, and we were only in court 15 minutes. At least we did that part right.

She rented a house about 45 minutes away from where I lived. I only saw my daughters on alternate weekends, for a couple of weeks over the summer, and a few days over the Christmas break. I felt like an uncle.

Residual resentment from 10 years of marriage, along with current resentments from being divorced, welled up inside of me. I hated paying child support, and I loathed hearing good or bad news about my daughters over the phone. Not surprisingly, I began to resist my divorce … and to avoid my commitments. I would show up a few minutes late every time I picked up the girls. Then, depending on which would be more inconvenient for Roberta, I would either drop them off a little early, or a bit late. I would do anything I could to make her life more difficult.

My resistance reached its peak when I began to manipulate the child support payments. I had agreed to pay child support every week, and of course I continued to never do anything "wrong" (self-righteousness is a terrific *Non-Survival Program*). I mailed each check on a Friday, so it would be post-marked before the deadline, but would not arrive until Monday or Tuesday. This, of course, was not my fault.

Roberta finally got really angry with me, so I told her she would get her checks by Saturday if I had to drive them to her house. I would ruin my own weekend by driving the check to her home and leaving it stuck in the door … about one minute before midnight (what a jerk I was).

Finally, after about 18 months of this nonsense, I got it. I really got it. I finally saw what I was doing. I still remember the feeling as I was writing a child-support check. I stopped as it hit me. "*You know,"* I thought, *"this is a lot of money. But, she used to get all of it. Now, I get to keep most of it.*" I smiled, and everything changed.

Suddenly, my attitude was completely different. Life the way it "is," became better than life the way it "isn't." I even had the thought, *"Besides, if I had to pay someone to take care of my daughters as well as Roberta does, I would never be able to afford it. Heck, this is actually pretty reasonable."*

It was then that I remembered my commitment to Roberta. When we got married, I made a promise before God, my family, and our friends to, *"Love, honor and <u>cherish</u>, until death do us part."*

I did not make that commitment conditional on how Roberta treated me. I did not even say I would cherish her unless she asked for a divorce. I said I would cherish Roberta until I died. I swore an oath to that … to God.

I never realized until that moment, the reason Roberta divorced me was because I destroyed the trust and the love. It began when I bastardized my own integrity the first time I criticized her instead of cherishing her (I probably did that on our wedding day). Over the years, I gave her countless reasons to distrust me. From Roberta's perspective, if I had lied about committing to cherish her "no matter what," then it was certainly possible that I had lied about loving her as well.

Roberta asked for the divorce, that much is true. However, I was the one who ended our marriage when I showed I could not be trusted.

> *"I promise to love, honor and cherish you, until death do us part."*
>
> I decided it was about time I kept my word.

I called Roberta and asked her if it would be OK if I would send her four (4) checks every month, each post-dated for its respective Saturday, so she never had to worry about when they would show up. She almost fainted. Cherishing Roberta again was going to be fun.

From that time on, I began using the Trust Formula. Every time she nagged or complained, under my breath I softly spoke, *"I honor you and I accept you, even though I don't understand you."*

However, I was not perfect and sometimes I did react. Later, when I realized what I had done, instead of beating myself I simply turned the Trust Formula inward and said, *"I honor myself and I accept myself, even when I don't understand myself."* The effects were staggering.

First and foremost, I stopped living with resentment. That alone was worth the efforts of using The Trust Formula. Then, Roberta started encouraging our daughters to spend more time with me.

Next, I got a lesson I was not expecting. I never realized how my anger for Roberta was affecting how other women perceived me. Within weeks of changing my attitude about Roberta, another incredible woman entered my life … Christine Gail Lesch. I probably would never have asked Roberta for a divorce, but since she had decided to divorce me, I was now free to pursue Christine. My divorce, which had become my curse, became my blessing. I was now able to date someone I would have been too unworthy to consider most of my life. Fortunately, for me, Christine and I were married later that same year.

To see just how much healing occurred, a few years later when Roberta and Harry Begley were about to be married, Christine and I were invited to their wedding. That may be common in some parts of the world, but it is rare in Chicago. Harry and I even posed for a photo together, to commemorate the last moment that, *"Neither one of us are married to Roberta."* However, what made me most proud is that Roberta asked my wife Christine to sing at her ceremony. That was pure class.

However, having a wife and a former wife, who get along with each other, does create some interesting moments. Such as the time I heard them trading stories about me, and laughing hysterically. Nevertheless, I would not trade our friendship for anything. Roberta has helped us out of two financial binds, and she was with my father when he died. She is still one of my best friends. I cannot take credit for the friendship, as we both share that. All I did was stop resenting, start giving, and allow her to give to me.

Postscript … Roberta's Response

Hi Ross:

I have just finished reading the section about you and me. I am deeply touched. Thank you. I wouldn't change a thing.

Perhaps someday I'll share my version of our story with you, however, I am guessing you already know a lot of it. I will always love you and I do cherish you and all that we have shared. Most of all our friendship and our daughters. Chris & your children rank high on my list, too. Not to mention your family.

And then there are all the memories. I basically grew up with you, most of my memories include you, and most of the funny stories I tell involve you. I have many 'Ross-isms' that are cherished parts of me. Most of all, I manage to make sure that just about everyone I meet and have an intimate conversation with knows that I am blessed to have an exceptional relationship with my first husband, his wife and children. Thank you.

Love, Roberta

Imagine a man freezing in an old log cabin
during a blizzard. Holding an armload of wood and
standing before a cold wood-stove, he shouts,
"Stove, I'll give you wood when you give me heat."

And he just stands there, freezing to death.
Holding on to the one thing that will save him.

When we wait to give until our boss gives
us a promotion, or our spouse gives us love …
just like that man in the cabin, we freeze to death.

Quit focusing on what you are going to get.
Focus on what you have to give.

Giving -- The Highest Blessing

Throughout history, only a handful of people have spent their lives giving unconditionally. Unfortunately, once you get past people such as Jesus Christ, Mahatma Gandhi, Mother Teresa, and Dr. Martin Luther King, Jr., the list drops off rather quickly.

For some people giving can be threatening, even without a negative circumstance. Leaders who give when things go wrong are a rarity. Most people justify their *Fear-Based* reactions regardless of the severity, or lack of severity, of the circumstance.

Mother Teresa created peace and joy in Calcutta. You and I have created problems at events designed to be celebrations … such as birthday parties and vacations. The question is: could we do better?

Forgiveness could be defined as, "To give forth love." Forgiveness may be the most powerful of all human expressions. Probably the best way to forgive is to decide to use The Trust Formula, but add a "Forgiveness" statement. When you are hurting or resentful simply think to yourself …

"I honor you and I accept you,
even though I don't understand you…
and I forgive you."

Or, as needed …

"I honor myself and I accept myself,
even though I don't understand myself…
and I forgive myself."

If you really want inner peace, quality relationships, and a successful career, quit focusing on what you are going to get, and instead focus on what you are going to give. When I make that statement in my seminars, I often hear someone remark *"I gave until I was used up,"* or *"I gave until I could give no more."* These and other similar comments indicate that giving drained the individual … which is untrue.

Think back to a time when you were shopping for a gift for a dear friend, and you found the perfect gift. You know, the kind of gift that was so perfect, you could not wait to see the expression on the face of the receiver?

You took it home and wrapped it with feelings of joy and anticipation. Then, when the gifts were being opened, you casually kept pushing it back out of the way until it was the last gift. Remember how you felt as you commented, *"Oh, here is one more gift."* Your smile was so big your friend knew something was up, and perhaps even looked at you and said, *"OK, what are you up to?"* as they opened their gift.

Now recall the gasp, scream, or laugh when your friend opened the package and said, *"Where did you find this, I can't believe it. It's just perfect!"* Rather than being drained or exhausted, you were energized, weren't you? You were smiling, laughing, crying, hugging, joyful, or excited. Giving creates energy.

> *"It isn't what you give,*
> *its how much love you put in the giving."*
>
> ... Mother Teresa

If however, your giving has a "hook" in it, it is not giving at all; it is selling. That can be exhausting. When giving is done "conditionally" there is a consequence. In most cases, the other person will respond in kind. They will also give conditionally. Eventually, trust is destroyed and the relationship ceases to exist, or at least ceases to be desirable.

When feeling resentment, however, giving is usually the last thing on our minds. Typical conditional thoughts and statements are ...

"I'll love you if you love me."
"I'll love you unless you fool around."
"I'll love you until you hurt me."

Comments such as these actually mean we are selling ourselves, not giving of ourselves. By so doing, we eventually begin to limit and destroy our own gifts.

In our professional lives these conditions change very little. In these relationships, the thoughts and statements may sound like …

"I won't quit if you give me a raise."
"I'll work hard unless you take advantage of me."
"I'll be loyal until you stop promoting me."

All of us have experienced giving or receiving unconditional love. Granted, some of us have experienced more than others, but we have all experienced at least some.

> *"Love in your heart wasn't put there to stay.*
> *Love isn't love 'til you give it away"*
>
> … Unknown

In your career, have you ever screwed up, but been given a second chance? Perhaps you forgave a friend for hurting you not because they treated you badly, but in spite of that fact. Maybe a fatigued parent chose to stay up all night caring for you when you were sick, despite needing sleep.

There is a quote from the Bible I have heard a hundred times in my life. *"It is more blessed to give than to receive"* (Acts 20:32). Nonetheless, as with most people, the truth was so obvious I missed it for a long time.

EXERCISE

QUESTION: If it really is *"more blessed to give than to receive"* … What is the highest thing you can do for another human being?

ANSWER:____

ANSWER BEFORE CONTINUING … NO CHEATING

QUESTION:

If it is *"more blessed to give than to receive"* …
What is the highest thing you can do for another human being?

ANSWER:

Allow them to give to you.
Allow others to have that *"highest blessing."*

Let other people have the highest blessing. It does not mean to take from them. Simply allow them to give to you. For example, when your 5-year old offers to make your bed … let her. Then, when it is done all wrong, do not belittle her or even correct her. Take pictures of your "imperfectly" made bed and stick them on the refrigerator. Put a big note under the photo that says something like, *"Kelly did this for me today."*

When we do not let others give to us, we take away the opportunity for them to receive the highest blessing. Perhaps you worry about what others might think of you, if it appears you are too weak to handle a problem yourself. Maybe you just do not want to be a burden. Often, you are busy and it is just quicker to do it yourself than to take the time to tell someone else how to do it. After all, something must be wrong with you if you need help … so for God's sake never actually ask for help.

Regardless, for you to demonstrate the *Four E's of Excellence* when challenged or threatened, you need to take a different approach. When you are hurting and someone asks if something is wrong … tell them. When someone asks if they can help you with something … let them. The excellent leader motivates others to give at home, at work, at places of worship, in the community, and globally.

The Widow

John and Mary lived the kind of relationship few of us have realized. They were in college when they first met. But, it was not a "love-at-first-sight" fairy tale. In fact, Mary's first impression of John was that he was obnoxious. John thought Mary was attractive, but stuck-up.

Because theirs was a small college, it was not uncommon for them to bump into each other. They were always cordial, but certainly not overly friendly with each other.

However, Mary's younger sister, Nancy, thought they would make a great couple. Nancy covertly tried to arrange meetings between them. She was unsuccessful at several attempts, but finally struck gold.

Nancy bought two tickets to a Chicago Cubs game, and asked John if he would like to go. John was not particularly interested in Nancy, but being a Cubbies fan he naturally accepted the invitation.

Nancy knew that her sister was a rabid Cubs fan. On the day of the game Nancy pretended to be sick and asked Mary to take her place at the game. Mary actually accused her sister of faking in order to finally get her and John on a date. It took several "sickly" denials but Mary relented and accepted the ticket. After all, she thought, everybody is a little obnoxious at a baseball game … so how bad could it be to go with John? Actually, pretty bad.

John refused to pay for a high priced parking spot near Wrigley Field, and by the time he finally found a spot the game was underway. The long walk meant that it was well into the second inning before they found their seats.

Mary was not happy. She was irritated that they had missed seeing the Cubs score in the bottom of the first inning. The situation did not improve when the Dodgers scored in each of the next few innings to take a commanding lead.

Trying to set things right, John went to get some hotdogs and beer. On his way up the stairs with the food, some kids bumped into John, causing him to spill everything all over himself.

Standing a couple of feet away from Mary, he ran his finger through the mustard and beer covering his shirt and put it in his mouth. Looking directly at her, John smiled and said … *It's delicious. Want a taste?"*

That is when it began. Mary thought John would explode with anger when the food was flung all over his clothing. Instead, she saw a confident humor that really stated, *"This is no big deal. I might as well have some fun."* In short, John melted Mary's icy barrier and she burst out laughing.

After that, John and Mary had a ball. They began by sharing their favorite Cubs stories, and ended up the day agreeing to go out on a real date. Two years later, they were married.

Over the years, John and Mary experienced all of the events that can adversely affect marriages: children, job problems, money problems, religious differences, and parental interference. But, each challenge only served to make them closer and more supportive of each other.

They rarely disagreed and never fought. Even though Mary tended towards the "appropriate" side, John's antics only brought her joy. Then the unthinkable happened.

Not long after their 46th anniversary, John was killed by a drunk driver. Somehow, with the help of her family, Mary managed to move her body through the ritual of John's funeral.

All most people could do when they approached her was to hug and say, *"I'm so sorry Mary. If you need anything, anything at all, please just call."*

Mary would politely say, *"Thank you, I will. Thanks for coming."*

> To Lead With Excellence is to Inspire Others to Give.

As I watched these exchanges, a thought came over me. The statement, *"If you need anything, please just call,"* has to be one of the safest offers of all time. The one thing most people in a similar situation are almost certain <u>not</u> to do … is call.

Over the next few weeks, people dropped by her house with casseroles and gifts. Little by little the attention waned, and Mary went into a world of survival and coping. But, her light slowly went out. Coping was not 'living.'

It was Nancy who saw that something had to be done. She tried taking her sister out to dinner, and inviting her over to play cards. Nothing worked. Finally, she got an idea.

A few weeks after the funeral, she made Mary a nice meal and took it to her home. Upon arrival Nancy said, *"Hi Hon, I just brought you a little something to freeze for a day when you don't want to cook."*

Then, in the kitchen as they made room for it in the freezer Nancy asked her sister, *"Oh. Could I ask you a favor? My church is having a bake sale and it would be a huge help if you could make a couple of dozen cookies for me to sell."*

Mary was still overwhelmed with grief and was withdrawing from life. There was not a chance she would ever ask for help of any kind. However, the one thing she could not do was to refuse the request of someone else who needed her help, especially her sister. She said yes.

This was the new beginning for Mary. After baking the cookies, and getting out of the house to deliver them to Nancy's church, she started visiting friends, going to movies, and even joined her sister's church. Soon, she was one of its most reliable volunteers. She never stopped grieving her loss of John, but she stopped letting the grief imprison her.

It is more blessed to give than to receive. Nancy's leadership created the space for Mary to experience some blessings at this traumatic time in her life, by choosing to give. The alternative of falling into a deep Freeze reaction never really took hold.

Relationship Excellence really breaks down
to just two things …

1) Choosing to be a giver.

2) Inspiring others to become givers.

"I Haven't Spoken To My Mother in 20 Years"

It was Sunday of a LifeStream Basic Seminar. The breakthroughs and insights were typically profound. A woman, about 45-years-old, came to the front of the room. Joan shared, *"I haven't spoken to my mother in 20 year's."*

She and her mother had fought over how she was raising her children. It was a bitter argument, and Joan was simply tired of fighting. Finally, she told her mother, *"Never call me again."*

My father asked Joan what she wanted. Her response was simple. *"I want my mother back."*

He told Joan, *"Go call her."*

I accompanied her to the pay phones, while everyone else took a break. I never saw anyone shake so severely. She could barely dial the phone.

It took a few minutes to connect. When I heard the words, *"Mother it's me, Joan."* I stepped away to give her privacy. She was sobbing already.

Joan was still on the phone when the break ended, so we began without her. A couple more people shared their insights and commitments. There were some intriguing stories. Then, Joan returned.

When she walked to the front of the room it was clear she was excited. Joan's smile went practically from ear to ear. She shared with us that she and her mother had cried together for the last 25 minutes, and shared regret and longing which both had been carrying for years. Joan had made a commitment to visit her mother the following weekend. She was glowing.

About 20 other people called their parents or children during that lunch break. It was an inspiring afternoon. Joan's courage affected people she would never meet. It was a terrific example of the impact of the *Four E's of Excellence* in action.

Later, Joan told us about the wonderful weekend she and her mother had shared. They visited, shopped, and toured Indianapolis together. One time they began crying and hugging while crossing the street. The light changed during their hug and a cop had to actually move them to the curb. It must have been like a scene from a movie.

Several days later, her mother was killed in an automobile accident. I saw Joan before she left for the funeral. I was amazed. She was completely at peace. Joan told me that, had she not reconciled with her mother, the accident would have probably killed her as well. Now, she could let her mother go. At the funeral, Joan re-connected with a few other long-lost relatives. Today, she no longer lives in isolation.

EXERCISE

Describe a time when another person forgave you for something, or created a solution to a problem of yours. Maybe a parent stayed up all night caring for you when you were sick, ignoring his or her own need for sleep.

Next, describe a time when you chose to give unconditional love when someone else had hurt you. Perhaps a co-worker got mad at you for something, but you chose to forgive, despite the hurt.

Now, describe a current negative circumstance where you are resenting another person. This can either be a person you cherish, or someone you hate. Game plan a response using the *Four E's of Excellence,* to prepare for your next encounter with their negativity.

Suggestion: Start small.

"Internal, Interpersonal, and International …
Our One Quest is Peace."

Chapter 10

The *Love-Based* Leader

The quest for peace is universal. Usually we seek an "internal" peace associated with physical wellness and self-worth. Often the quest is for "interpersonal" peace, created from having fulfilling personal and business relationships. There is also a longing for "international" peace, which comes from living in a world where mutual respect exists between nations.

In most cases the motivating factor for this quest is fear, whether the threat is real or perceived. By overcoming *Fear-Based* reactions with the *Four E's of Excellence,* you can significantly increase your chances for creating peace ... personally, professionally, and globally.

Love-Based Leadership

The process of making a positive difference,
and inspiring others, by maintaining self-control.

When I first introduced the concept of *Love-Based* leadership in a business seminar, one of the reactions was, *"Love-Based Leader? In business? There is no love in business."* I was reminded of Tom Hanks in "A League of Their Own," when he said, *"Are you crying? There's no crying in baseball."* Nonetheless, many baseball players have cried during a game. Even tough guy Pete Rose has cried on the field.

There is also love in business. I always felt fortunate when I had a job that I loved. Whenever I was in a sales position, if I made a sale I really loved my new client. I really did. Any time I was promoted to a higher-paying job, I always loved it. Several of my clients, and many former co-workers, have become close friends with whom genuine love and affection continue.

I could go on, but the concept is described more eloquently by Kahlil Gibran and Mother Teresa ...

> *"My work is my love made visible."*
>
> … Kahlil Gibran, The Prophet

My mother was fortunate to have been able to spend time with Mother Teresa. While at lunch, she asked her … *"Mother, what does prayer mean to you?"* Interestingly, her answer was somewhat similar to Gibran's:

> *"Prayer is work in action, and work in action is prayer."*
>
> … Mother Teresa

Most people did not see Mother Teresa as a businesswoman. Do not doubt it for a second. She was the head of a wonderful organization, The Sisters of Charity, which still depends solely on contributions inspired by Mother Teresa.

It is important to realize when we truly love our work, we are giving love. You do not have to be Mother Teresa to give love in your vocation. You can heal and bring joy to others with a cup of coffee and a kind word, by mending broken fenders or by creating artwork or music that brings joy and pleasure to the lives of others. Providing goods and services that others need to survive is itself a form of love.

A lot of giving in the corporate world is conditional (*"I'll work harder if I get a raise."*), and/or *Fear-Based ("If I speak up at the meeting, I'll get fired.").* The same is true in personal relationships. Giving is often conditional *(I'll love you if … "),* and/or *Fear-Based ("I can't go. So-and-so will throw a fit if I don't clean up this mess.").* Such "giving" is not loving. It is not even close. *Love-Based* leadership requires a higher standard, a change in thinking.

The concept of *Love-Based* leadership became clear to me while I was teaching a leadership seminar in Cincinnati. One of the participants shared the following story:

A Lesson in *Love-Based* Leadership

She was the kind of daughter parents dream of. She was talented, lovely, athletic, intelligent, joyful, and full of dreams for her life. Tragically, she was brutally murdered.

Her parents died more than a little bit themselves that day. In an attempt to cope, they turned her bedroom into a shrine filled with photographs, trophies, newspaper articles, art projects, and other memorabilia. Unfortunately, this monument served only to intensify their grief.

A few months later, the girl's mother had a startling insight. She asked her husband, *"If we'd raised a son who could have done such a thing to another person, just imagine the pain we'd be going through right now."* Unbelievably, she and her husband went to the parents of their daughter's killer … to help them deal with their own grief and shame.

> We may have no control over our negative circumstances, but...
>
> we have total control over ourselves,
> and how we handle those circumstances.

The deceased girl's mother created a healing connection with people whom most of us would have resented, avoided, or even attacked. She even influenced her husband to participate in this choice. Realizing they could not change their circumstance (and would have found it nearly impossible to forgive the man who killed their daughter), these people instead chose to create a new circumstance in which they could be loving and giving. What a powerful and beautiful legacy for their daughter.

Benjamin Franklin changed a habit every 21 days. Maxwell Maltz, in his book Psychocybernetics, reported it takes 21 days to change a habit or belief. Attending a weekend seminar, or reading a book, can only have temporary effects … unless you practice and demonstrate the tools and lessons you have learned for at least 21 days. When developing the skills of *Love-Based* leadership, I suggest you start small, and celebrate "little" victories … then tackle bigger challenges.

Friendly Fred

My first exposure to *Love-Based* leadership occurred as a teen in Thousand Oaks, California. My parents, James and Janet Quinn, were successful business owners. My father was president of the Merchant's Association, a member of The Chamber of Commerce, and sat on the Board of Directors of California Lutheran College. My mother was president of a large Republican women's club. They also belonged to many other recreational, civic, and charitable organizations.

The natural consequence of their activities and friendships was a steady stream of people through our home. Add three teenagers (Nancy, Gary, and me) plus our friends and you can see why our house was referred to as the Quinn "circus."

> *"Love thy neighbor as thyself."* ... Leviticus 19:18
>
> Based on how most people love themselves,
> our neighbors are in serious trouble.

While ours was one of the most visited houses in town, I do not recall anyone ever visiting next door. This was the home of Mr. and Mrs. Fred Nichols. Fred was the most unfriendly man I have ever known.

Every morning his garage door would open and Fred would leave for work. Every evening it would swallow him up. Fred so desired isolation he created a two-fence barrier between himself and his five backyard neighbors. Apparently, Fred did not feel just one fence was enough, because he actually built a second fence about one foot inside of the original. We jokingly nicknamed him "Friendly Fred."

Friendly Fred's one love (hopefully in addition to his wife) was his beautiful dicondra lawn. Dicondra lawns are always green and never need mowing. However, they need lots of sun and water. Southern California is blessed with lots of sun, but not much rain. To compensate, Friendly Fred watered his precious dicondra daily. The result was squishy ground ... so squishy you would leave an impression if you stepped on his lawn.

About the only times we saw Friendly Fred was when he came outside to water his lawn, or to yell at us kids for playing football in the street, or for riding our bikes on his sidewalk. He was afraid we might damage his property.

If you have ever seen how teenagers can rebel against anyone who tries to enforce authority, then you know his fears were valid. We would purposely leave impressions on his lawn since aggravating this man proved to be more enjoyable than any football game.

Due to Friendly Fred's quick temper, he became the butt of jokes and nasty comments by adults and teens alike. We made fun of his negativity without giving a second thought to how much negativity we were creating by our treatment of him.

Friendly Fred also resented anyone who parked in front of his house because they would step on his lawn while exiting their cars. This resentment led to one of my greatest life lessons.

Since it was not always possible to find a parking space in front of the Quinn circus, occasionally one of our visitors would park in front of Friendly Fred's home. Fred would rush out so quickly to yell at them, we figured he must sit by his window just waiting for his chance to bolt outside and explode on any unsuspecting victim.

Friendly Fred might have been unfriendly, but he wasn't stupid. He bought a sprinkler, which sprayed water on his lawn and way out into the street. *"Now,"* he must have thought, *"nobody will park here."*

This worked like a charm, and nobody parked in front of Friendly Fred's house when he was watering. However, since he could not water his lawn all of the time, those people who parked there when the sprinkler was off would still get his hostile reaction.

One time, Friendly Fred chose to water his lawn after several cars had already parked in front of his house. When my brother and I noticed what he was doing, we started to get angry. My father reminded us of one of his favorite sayings:

> *"When life gives you lemons, make lemonade."*

Instead of getting angry, we decided to have a little fun at Friendly Fred's expense. My brother and I got a chamois cloth and washed our friends' cars with his water.

Apparently, Friendly Fred failed to see the humor in this, and he came out and yelled at us. We simply laughed at him to rub salt in his wounds. It went on like this for several years.

One day my parents were throwing a large party. They did not want trouble from Friendly Fred, so the invitations clearly warned everyone not to park in front of his house. Guests parked in front of other people's houses up and down the street. We were certain we would have a pleasant afternoon without having to deal with Friendly Fred.

It was a typical California summer day, hot and sunny. Most of the people were in the back yard cooking, eating and drinking. Some people were playing croquet and ping-pong while others were inside preparing food or shooting pool. Everyone was having a marvelous time.

However, one friend was late for the party. Bill had just returned from a trip and had spent the morning taking delivery of his dream car, a Cadillac convertible destined to be a classic.

Bill was so excited to show off his new car that he drove straight to our party without checking his mail. He never read the invitation with the parking warning, so he pulled his car into the only remaining space; smack in front of Friendly Fred's house.

Bill joined the party and played the *"Guess what I did today"* game with us. After about an hour he told us and we hurried out front to see his new car.

To our collective horror we saw his beautiful Cadillac convertible, with the top down, being soaked by Friendly Fred's sprinkler. Apparently, Friendly Fred had decided it was a good time to water his lawn. He had sprayed Bill's new car with water for almost an hour.

My dad took one look and exploded. In my 17 years, I had never seen him this angry. My father was so furious he could not even talk. He leapt over the little hedge separating our front yards, and ran across Friendly Fred's dicondra lawn kicking out big divots of the wet sod with each step.

When my father got to the sprinkler, he kicked it so hard he broke his toe. Now, however, instead of shooting water into Bill's Cadillac, the spray was directed into Friendly Fred's open bedroom window.

We moved Bill's car into our driveway and dried it out. There was surprisingly little damage. This, however, did not cool down my father.

Friendly Fred had called the police. He wanted my dad arrested for wrecking his lawn, breaking his sprinkler and soaking his drapes. Because of dad's community involvement, both officers knew my father so he was not arrested. They got him to return to the party while they dealt with Friendly Fred, but my father was still extremely angry.

The party lost its joyousness, and people soon departed. My father ranted all night about how he was going to get even with Friendly Fred.

The next day my father could not work because of his anger. He decided to come home early and make himself a drink. This is a man who never came home early, rarely got angry, and never got drunk. Yet there he sat, drinking in our family room with his anger increasing each minute.

About 5:30, we saw Friendly Fred drive past our house and get swallowed into his garage. I was worried my father might go next door and start a fight.

A few minutes later, Friendly Fred was coming up our sidewalk. He rang the bell and my dad opened the door. I was certain a fight was about to break out until I saw that Friendly Fred was crying. He looked at my dad and said, *"Jim, I just wanted to come over to apologize for yesterday."*

My father was visibly confused. *"Apologize?"*

Fred, crying, continued, *"… and to thank you for the flowers."*

"Flowers?" my dad asked, really confused now.

Fred, oblivious to my dad's confusion, was holding a small card and he read from it out loud, *"Isn't it silly for people to act this way? We really do love you."*

Fred was actually sobbing as he read. When he finished, Fred handed the card to my father who then read it to himself …

Dear Fred,

Isn't it silly for people to act this way?
We really do love you.

Jim & Jan

Fred then said through his tears, *"Thank you Jim. I want you to know this is the first time in my life anyone has sent me flowers."*

My father continued reading the card trying to figure out what was going on, and then I saw him smile. As I found out later, he realized what had happened. In an attempt to solve the problems with our neighbor, my mother had sent flowers and a nice card to Friendly Fred.

But there was more. She had signed the card *"**Jim** & Jan."* My mother knew my father would probably object to this *Love-Based* solution, and would have certainly refused to allow her to sign his name, so she said nothing to him about her little gift.

Fred kept speaking, *"Jim, I was really touched by the flowers, and I can't tell you how much I appreciated getting them. But I really came over to thank you for something else."* He took the card back from my father and read aloud again. *"Isn't it silly for people to act this way? We really do love you."*

Still crying, he managed to continue: *"I had to come and tell you how important it is to me what you wrote on this card. I want you to know, except for my wife, you are the only people in my life who have* <u>*ever*</u> *told me they love me."*

Fred broke down in sobs. My dad just held him in his arms, and neither said a word for several minutes. We had spent years making fun of Friendly Fred, when the only thing he really needed was our love.

From that day onward, whenever anyone asked my father how to handle a difficult person, his response was always the same:

> *"Just give them love ...*
> *Just give them love ...*
> *Just give them love."*

Develop *Love-Based* Leadership by Starting Small

Over the years, as I taught people how to create solutions to their personal and professional problems, I realized there was something deeper to be explored. Every time someone chose to overcome a *Fear-Based* reaction, the effort inspired others. While these actions rarely inspired everyone, and in fact often failed to reach even the intended person, they always inspired someone. Always.

The best definition of a leader is someone who inspires others. Further investigation reveals these inspirations to be the automatic result of positive solutions to any negative situations, large or small. So, instead of a traditional workshop teaching leadership "skills," I simply taught people how to overcome their own negative reactions to small negative circumstances. They barely noticed they became leaders in the process.

Fear-Based reacting is a habit. *Four E's of Excellence* can also become a habit. Start small. Build your competency as a *Love-Based* leader.

Two Flowers

When I challenge my students to use the *Four E's of Excellence* to create *Love-Based* solutions at work, there is usually some resistance. True, some people fear rejection … but even that is often just an excuse for not trying. Many times they simply lack an idea they can get enthusiastic about. The solution is to use small groups to come up with a consensus idea for each team member.

> *"It's not about doing great things.*
> *It's about doing small things with greatness."*
>
> … Mother Teresa

The best ideas are usually simple. They stand out with their elegance. If you are stuck for an idea, the solution is to form a small group to come to consensus on an idea. For example, one man told his team he disliked how personal relationships tended to stay within each department. Each, in fact, seemed to have become a little island unto itself. Accounting ate together, as did shipping, personnel, computer processing, and the rest of the departments in his location. Everyone ate with the same people they worked with, even though they ate in the same lunchroom at the same time. Even the sales department, when they were not having lunch with clients, tended to eat with each other.

One of the members of his team suggested an idea. He laughed, and then decided to do it.

That night he bought two flowers on his way home. In the morning, he got to work early and placed a flower on the desk of someone in Quality Control, and one flower on a desk in Accounting. The next day he placed a flower on the desk of the Vice-President's secretary, and one in a work-station in computer processing.

This process continued for days. He would arrive early and place a flower on a different desk in two different departments. By the end of the first week, both people who received a flower were actively trying to find out who got the other one. By the end of the second week, everyone was arriving in the lunchroom in anticipation of discovering who got flowers that day.

Lunchtime became a joyous time of mingling and laughter.

Once, he even put a flower on his own desk, to avert suspicion. He continued for about a month, and was never identified. After he quit bringing flowers, he noticed that people continued to look for the recipients of that day's flowers. People were starting to miss the event.

One day he got to work and found that several of the previous recipients had gotten together and purchased a flower for everybody. They had bought dozens of flowers and placed one on every desk, work-station, locker, and truck. People were more excited than when bonuses were handed out.

Lunch was never the same again. People are still trying to figure out who the "flower-person" was. Every now and then, he comes early and drops off another two flowers. Periodically, so do others. On more than one occasion, he has come to work to find a flower on his own desk.

He will never talk. He is having too much fun. So is everyone else.

> *"Man is the center of a circle, the circumference of which is determined by self-imposed limitations."*
>
> … Mahatma Gandhi

Are people fighting to get into your life, or are they fighting to get out of it? Are you moving closer to global impact or closer to solitary confinement?

Growing as a *Love-Based* Leader

I have often used Mother Teresa as an example of an excellent leader. People admire many different facets of her persona. For some it is her faith. For others it is her love for, and commitment to, *"the poorest of the poor."* By studying her, many have learned to emulate and demonstrate these qualities.

However, there is often a negative, side effect. Sometimes people admire her so much, they cannot see her qualities in themselves. They actually say things such as, *"She is incredible. But, I could never do what she does*."

People who make such statements actually diminish their own self-worth. They also belittle the actual effort of the honored person, who had to overcome his or her own challenges and self-doubts.

It is ironic that the very act of praising a great person should have a limiting effect on the person giving the acknowledgement. When people are "awed" by someone, they may engage in philosophical discussions about the person's qualities or accomplishments. However, because most believe they cannot reach the same level of accomplishment, they do not even try.

> *"When you put someone on a pedestal,*
> *you are really putting yourself into a hole."*
>
> … Jan Quinn Sanders (my mother)

No two people see exactly the same qualities in another person. It is not possible to recognize a great quality, unless you yourself possess elements of that quality. It goes under the, *"It takes one to know one"* theory, also known as the 'mirror concept.' If you truly want to discover your gifts and talents, seek out within yourself that which you admire in another.

Martin Luther King Jr., is an excellent example to use with the mirror concept. Some people admired his determination. For others it was his compassion. Many saw Dr. King's speaking ability as his greatest attribute, and others saw it as his commitment to non-violent protest. Determine the characteristic you admire, and then strive to develop it yourself.

Fear-Based reactors justify negative behaviors when they are afraid. Whether by Fight, Flight, Freeze, or Facade they strive to control others. Their attitude to others is, "*You are the problem. If you would just change what you are doing, then there would be no problem."* In essence, they seek to create peace by trying to make others responsible for solving problems.

Conversely, *Love-Based* leaders choose to respond using the *Four E's of Excellence.* With Ethics, Enthusiasm, Evaluation, and Empathy; they maintain self-control when afraid. Their attitude to others is, *"I don't understand you, but I do understand that if you were not threatened, you would not be reacting. It is in my own best interest to change whatever it is I am doing (or am perceived as doing), and thus remove the threat."* They seek to create peace by being responsible for solving problems themselves.

Notice both groups are interested in the same result. However, by trying to control others, *Fear-Based* reactors are losing effectiveness. The irony is, by taking control of their own lives, *Love-Based* leaders are having a greater impact on others than they ever dreamed possible.

The Dachau Survivor

In 1982, I attended a lecture in Evanston, Illinois, which had a profound impact on my view of forgiveness as a tool for peace. The speaker was famous for his "forgiveness" messages, so most of the people in attendance were already supportive of this topic. It promised to be an inspirational evening for people who were quite open to his concepts. This was not a hostile crowd.

An impromptu survey of several people revealed I was one of the few in the audience who had not read any of the speaker's books. To remedy this situation, I went to the lobby and bought one. I thought that, perhaps, I would be able to have it autographed.

The speaker came out to a rousing ovation, and spoke on the power of love and forgiveness for more than an hour. He would have us in tears one moment, then laughing a few minutes later. He spoke beautifully and effortlessly. Everyone was having a marvelous time.

Firmly he stated, *"You have to forgive your enemies, and you have to forgive family members who've hurt you. You have to forgive strangers, as well as yourself. Forgiveness is the key to peace and happiness."* People were practically cheering. So far, so good.

The speaker was doing well, until he said something rarely heard in a public address. He said, *"In fact, the Jews will never be free until they forgive Hitler."*

Our celebration of good feelings hit a wall and there was an abrupt silence. You could hear a collective gasp of disbelief at what had just been spoken, followed by an "explosion" of vehemence, the likes of which I have never witnessed.

As he spoke the words, *"In fact, the Jews will never be free until they forgive Hitler,"* a tiny woman in the third or fourth row stood up and started screaming at him. Her tirade was a mixture of profanity, insults, and tears. It was quite difficult to decipher, but what I could understand sent a chill down my spine.

It became apparent that she was a survivor of the Dachau concentration camp. It was clear her hatred for Nazis would not tolerate any attempt to diminish her resentment and loathing.

She lived in nearby Skokie. Many survivors of concentration camps settled in this community after World War II. There were probably several other Holocaust survivors in the audience, and many of their children. This was not the place to say, *"In fact, the Jews will never be free until they forgive Hitler."*

For several minutes, she spat her hatred at the speaker, and then literally collapsed from exhaustion into the arms of the people sitting next to her. She was totally spent.

I had been watching the speaker during her attack. Never had I seen a man so naked before. He just stood there and took it. You could see the depth of compassion on his face. I watched him struggle to find something, anything, to say to her. Of course, there was nothing he could say to help her.

He knew this woman really needed to forgive for her own sake. However, any response on his part such as, *"Hating the Nazis is killing you,"* or *"Forgiveness is divine,"* would sound like an empty platitude, and he knew it.

His mind appeared to be racing through thoughts. His presentation was destroyed as, apparently, he could not find the words and had nowhere to go. He simply stood there looking compassionately at the woman, as she tried to regain her breath.

Then, I heard someone crying. This was the only sound in the theatre of stunned listeners, and it began to attract attention.

A young man was standing and weeping uncontrollably. For a few moments I wondered about what he might do. Finally, he spoke through his tears … with a thick German accent. If I live to be a thousand, I hope I never forget what he said that evening.

He began softly and with compassion. *"Ma'am. Nobody has a right to hate more than you do. I can't imagine the horrors you've lived through. I can't imagine anybody treating another human in the ways you and others were treated. What makes it worse for me, however, is you are literally speaking of my parents and grandparents. It shames me as a German. Nobody has a right to hate more than you do."*

"But," and he pointed at the speaker and continued quite firmly, *"you must listen to this man. I have been having the Holocaust shoved down my throat since I was a child. I have been made to feel guilty and responsible. It has made me angry because I was not alive when those atrocities occurred."*

"I am not alone," he continued. *"Thousands, perhaps millions of other young Germans are fed up with being judged for acts that were committed by others. If it keeps up, they will react. You did not deserve to be treated the way you were treated, and we have not deserved to be made to feel guilty for it. Keep on hating … Hitler would approve."*

With that, he made his way through the crowd toward the woman. When he reached her, they embraced. The speaker visibly sighed with relief.

I watched as people reached in to hug the people, who were hugging the people, who were hugging the two of them. I would have given anything to be a part of that hug, but I was too far away.

However, the speaker was being ignored. So I went up on stage, and had him autograph my copy of his book.

Finally, he got everyone to take their seats and spoke some beautiful words, bringing closure to what we had all witnessed. However, I knew it was the words of this young man I would always remember …

> *"Keep on hating ... Hitler would approve."*

The Global *Love-Based* Leader

Over the last 30 years, there has been a global shift in leadership effectiveness. Managers, executives, parents, spouses, teachers, community leaders, elected officials, and other *Position-Based* leaders are increasingly frustrated because the old 'solutions' are not working.

Sometimes the problems are so overwhelming it can be easy to demonstrate one or more of the four *Fear-Based* reactions. However, whether it is Fight, Flight, Freeze or Facade, the one certainty is you become the problem when you are reacting because it gives others an excuse to react to you.

There are times when something so devastating occurs, you cry out for someone to take action. However, when you feel a fire in your belly about the 'wrongness' of an incident, and all you do is react, you have bastardized your own integrity. You have the chance to become part of the solution only if you choose to lead with love.

> *"Man must evolve for all human conflict, a method, which rejects revenge, aggression, and retaliation.*
>
> *The foundation of such a method is love. I believe that unarmed truth and unconditional love will have the final word in reality."*
>
> ... Martin Luther King, Jr.

Worldwide, we are desperately in need of leaders. Not controlling *Fear-Based* reactors, but Global *Love-Based* leaders. Fear makes a poor foundation for the choice of 'right' and 'wrong.' The only chance for peace to prevail is through the practice of the *Love-Based* qualities of Ethics, Enthusiasm, Evaluation, and of course, Empathy.

To many, the concept of *Love-Based* leadership sounds like pleasant philosophy. The perception is, anyone who strives to live up to this ideal will be walked on in relationships, taken advantage of in business, and ridiculed (or worse) on the global stage.

Great leaders such as Jesus Christ, Mother Teresa, Buckminster Fuller, Martin Luther King, Jr., Dr. Albert Schweitzer, Mahatma Gandhi, St. Francis of Assisi, and others have demonstrated the powerful alternative of *Love-Based* leadership. We have studied, honored, praised, and even worshiped the few who have lived this truth. Unfortunately, we have seldom made efforts to emulate them.

There are two reasons for this: First, the very effectiveness of such distinguished lives seems to elevate each of these 'saints' to a higher stature above us 'normal' people. Indeed, it almost feels arrogant to imagine ourselves being able to accomplish results in such a *Love-Based* manner.

Second, these people have always paid a penalty for their successes. They have toiled alone against impossible odds. They have been criticized and ridiculed. Many have been imprisoned or attacked … and some have even been killed. These prices, or even the possibility of them, are too high for most people to accept.

Position-Based leaders generally view *Love-Based* solutions as naïve, ineffective, foolhardy, and even dangerous. As a result, *Fear-Based* reactions abound. *"I don't get mad, I get even,"* has practically become our mantra.

Yes, there is a risk in choosing *Love-Based* leadership. However, there is a greater risk for failing to do so. The time has come to take the 'saints' off their pedestals. It is an insult to honor these people, while refusing to walk in their footsteps.

> We can no longer afford the luxury
> of relegating *Love-Based* leadership to the few.

Most people have learned how to fight <u>against</u> something, but few have learned how to fight <u>for</u> something … especially when threatened. Some people are gung-ho to fight terrorists, while others are attacking the people who support the war. 'Peace-Nicks' and 'War-Mongers,' as they un-affectionately label each other, have one thing in common ... they are both *Fear-Based* in their attacks on each other.

What effects are *Fear-Based* reactions having on Post-9/11 America, and the rest of the world? Is the movement more toward Oneness or Separation? Acceptance or Judgment? Love or Hate? Peace or War?

You have always known the truth. You have heard the concepts presented in this book in many ways …

"Do unto others as you would have them do unto you."
... The Golden Rule. Jesus, Matthew 7:12

"We are but strands in the web of life.
Whatsoever we do to the web, we do to ourselves."
... Chief Seattle

"What is hateful to you, do not do to your neighbor."
... Judaism -- Hillel, Talmud, Shabbat 31a

"For every action there is an equal and opposite reaction."
... Sir Isaac Newton

"Not one of you truly believes
until you wish for others what you wish for yourself."
... Islam -- The Prophet Muhammad, Hadith

"Treat not others in ways that you yourself would find hurtful."
... Buddhism -- The Buddha, Udana-Varga 5.18

"When you hurt someone else, you hurt yourself even more."
... Your Grandmother

"Do not do to others what would cause pain if done to you."
... Hinduism -- Mahabharata 5:1517

"Do not do to others what you do not want done to yourself."
... Confucianism -- Confucius, Analects 15:23

"And in the end the, love you take is equal to the love you make."
... The Beatles, Lennon & McCartney, Abbey Road

Finally, I contribute ...

And in the end, the hate you take is
equal to the hate <u>you</u> make.

If you think this equation is out of balance, then you are not dealing with reality. I challenge you to overcome your *Fear-Based* reactions with the *Four E's of Excellence*. You can be a *Love-Based* leader.

Whatever the question may be, hatred is not the answer. In the face of *Fear-Based* resentment, judgment, prejudice, vengeance, and war, *Love-Based* leadership can really sound simplistically naïve. Let's face it, *"All You Need Is Love,"* is wonderful ONLY when everyone else is being loving.

However, it is important to note that while *Love-Based* leaders do not react when threatened, they are not pacifists. Mother Teresa was a warrior. She fought her battles with love.

Love-Based leaders are needed in communities, where *Fear-Based* reactions are decimating families. There is an urgent need for corporate *Love-Based* leaders. The greed of executives in companies such as Enron, WorldCom, and Arthur Anderson has produced an increasingly *Fear-Based* economy. Most significantly, all acts of terrorism and reactions to those acts are *Fear-Based*. They have created an unprecedented need for *Global Love-Based* leaders.

A Sense of Urgency

Throughout history there have been those who became *Love-Based* leaders in spite of great obstacles, and who continue to affect the lives of others long after their deaths. Perhaps you have known some *Love-Based* leaders who, while not famous, inspired you in some fashion before they passed away … perhaps a friend or a relative. All of these people have something in common with one another, and eventually with you and me...

> Life is simply not long enough.
> There is NEVER enough time to get the job done.

There are no guarantees in life. Whether you only survive another five minutes, or live another 100 years, the only valid question is *"What are you going to do with the time you have left?"*

My son Shaunessy was born 6-weeks premature. He was so small and fragile we had to leave him in the hospital for several weeks. When we were finally allowed to take him home, I remember my mother holding him in her hands (and she has small hands). She looked up at me with a tear in her eye and said, *"This was you … just a heartbeat ago."* Time passes so quickly. Cherish each day.

There is a penalty for choosing to live as a *Fear-Based* reactor. Your dreams die a little bit each time you react negatively. As a result, most people kill their own dreams long before they die. When they get to the end of such a life, they have regrets, resentment, and blame. They know they never achieved their true potential. Is this your destiny?

Merely discussing and philosophizing what you have read will be a waste of time. Take action. In the words of my father, *"Given the opportunity, most people are prone to procrastinate."* Do it now. Possibly the greatest of all personal tragedies is to end your life with the thought, *"If only I had another chance."* Based on the number of chances most people waste, another life would make little difference.

However, there is also a penalty for choosing to overcome your issues and *Fear-Based* reactions and lead with excellence as a *Love-Based* leader. If you are unaware of this penalty you will be surprised and threatened when it occurs; and it will occur. To be aware of this penalty is to be prepared for it.

The penalty for leading with excellence, regardless of your motivation, is that you will be criticized when you fail, and you will be criticized when you succeed. You may be ridiculed for your great dreams or new ideas. Some people will misinterpret your good intentions, and will reject you. Before you begin, ask yourself a question. *"Can I handle some rejection?"*

If not, if acceptance by others is your only goal, then do not strive to be a *Love-Based* leader. Your reality of *Fear-Based* living will prevent it anyway, because approval-seeking is a full-time occupation.

However, if you truly wish to make an impact with your life far greater than you ever imagined, then the path of *Love-Based* leadership will empower you to manifest your dreams.

Your dreams give your life value.
But, it is how you live that gives your dreams value.

You will know the truth. When you die, you will know the world is a little better off because you lived. It will not matter to you if anyone else knows. You will know. With this knowledge, you will rest in peace. **But, there is another reason you need a sense of urgency …**

Fear-Based living is a thing of the past.
Control-Based leaders are history.

Love-Based leadership is the way of the future.

The Leadership Evolution

Few realize how the world changed forever in 1976. There is now enough of everything, for everyone. Buckminster Fuller calculated that we are doing so much more with so much less, that every single human living on Spaceship Earth is now able to live as only billionaires have lived in the past.

All children born after 1976 (and perhaps even those born a bit before that) are unique in history. They are experiencing the World from the 'enough for everyone' perspective. But, they have been raised by well-meaning pre-1976 parents, with a 'not enough for everyone' consciousness. They need model *Love-Based* leaders to show them the way. This is critical because they are about to raise the most powerful generation of leaders the world has ever seen.

It will be <u>their</u> children which represent another 'Baby Boom.' Not the population boom of Post World War II, but the 'Leadership Boom' of children born of Post-1976 parents. It will be far more profound than what was experienced in the 1960's.

These are, and will be, the first people to have been raised by parents who lived in a world where there is enough of everything for everyone. They will generally see the only obstacle left for world peace is in the thinking of the pre-1976 *Fear-Based* controllers of the past.

> The World has enough victims.
> We need *Love-Based* leaders … NOW.
>
> You are needed to pave the way for the first
> entire generation of potential *Love-Based* leaders.
>
> They should be making their presence felt about 2020.

The shift of human consciousness is near. The Leadership Evolution will occur with you or without you. It will be quicker and easier with you. Now is the time to teach these concepts, by putting them into action. Strive to create excellence WITH your life, not just IN your life. Do it now.

The Children Are Watching

Request For Leadership Stories

Stories of *Love-Based* leadership and *Four E's of Excellence* are being collected for future publication. Whether you have created a *Love-Based* solution to a negative circumstance, or witnessed one, please send us the details. These stories can be personal, relationship, family, professional, community, national, or global in nature.

The leadership effect of these events will continue to expand if others have the opportunity to identify and learn from each of them. Please send your stories to …

Quinn Incorporated

Four E's of Excellence

P.O. Box 851
W. Dundee, IL 60118-0851 U.S.A.

Quinn@ControllingOthers.com

http://www.ControllingOthers.com

Stories, once submitted, become the property of Quinn Incorporated and cannot be returned. If multiple entries are received for the same event, the entry with earliest postmark will be used.

The Author

James Roswell Quinn

"Ross" was born in Seattle, Washington in 1950. He grew up in the Los Angeles area and graduated from the University of Southern California, with a B.S. in Business Administration, in 1972.

In 1973, Quinn's parents, James and Janet Quinn, founded LifeStream. This seminar company assisted people in their personal and professional development. Ross moved to Chicago to join his parents in 1979, and has personally presented over 1,200 keynote speeches, workshops, and seminars. Together, they have taught in excess of 2,500 seminars, reaching more than 150,000 participants in United States, Canada, Israel, and New Zealand.

Quinn's corporate seminar, *"Four E's of Excellence"* (formally *The People Wheel),* has been presented to dozens of businesses and organizations worldwide. His clients include Walt Disney Feature Animation, the Toronto Real Estate Board, Nightingale-Conant Corporation, the Auckland Multiple Listing Bureau, and many others. In this workshop, participants learn how to communicate more effectively, thus creating a more positive work environment with reduced conflict; improved customer service; better use of available resources; faster time-to-market; and less employee turnover.

For 35 years, Ross has inspired participants from around the world to make a greater contribution with their lives. His leadership retreat utilizes high ropes 'confidence' courses, studies of Mother Teresa and Buckminster Fuller, as well as indoor and outdoor group activities designed to assist people desiring to increase their leadership skills. When this seminar is held in New Zealand, there are bonus adventures such as touring Hobbiton, swimming with dolphins, black-water rafting (through underground caverns), white water rafting, and bungy jumping.

Ross, and his wife Christine, developed the *Conscious Couples* weekend to help people create more effective and committed intimate relationships. The premise? … Troubled couples need joy, not work.

Whether in a keynote, workshop, or rock climbing, Quinn's leading-edge human development technology empowers people to overcome stress-related *Fear-Based* reactions, breakthrough non-productive behaviors, develop trust, and create consensus … in order to achieve their goals and dreams.

Ross is the father of six … Kelcey, Jancy, Carly, Shaunessy, Delaney, and Shanairra. He and Christine live in Sleepy Hollow, Illinois.

Acknowledgements

All of the following people have contributed to the *Controlling Others for Love and Profit.* Without their stories, editing, feedback, financial backing, love, support, and encouragement, quite simply … this book would not exist.

Thank you Peter Comrie, for without you I would not have begun. To Sandra Pierce, and George & Susan Buckley-Watson, your backing started a cascade of support, which the 'experts' said should have been impossible.

Thank you Jennifer Kaia Bartok, Janet Battaglio, Rudy Bazelmans, Regina Blake, Ross & Annette Bradbury, David Bryan, Darlene Buckingham, Emily Cieslinski, Rob Cleverly, Angie Coleman, Nancy & Jim Cooper (my sister and her husband), Jackie Cowan, Linda Cowan, Paul & Nancy Cushman, Aida & Michael Dennehy, Lina DiSanto, Wade Domet, Mark Doyle, Tom & Shirley Dusmet, Josie & Alan Estill, Karen Evans, JoAnne & Sam Feil, Kate & Michael Ferguson, Cally Field, Bobby Fielding, Beverly & Bill Gleason, Roger & Jackie Grey-Moores, Steve Guizzetti, Nan Hanna-Paquin, Michell Hays, Cindy Hoy, Craig & Barbara Imrie, Anne James, Lee Jeavons, Jillian Jeffery, Phil & Brenda Johnson, George Kaufman, Lila Keller, Shannon Kelly, Faye Kendel, Andre Kennedy, Kathleen & Jon Kores, Brenda Lawrie, Irv & Dorothy Lesch (my wife's parents), Sharon Lilla, Amy May, Nancy May, Jan McCormick, Rena Gaile & James Morgan, Karina Dagher & John Nemanic, Jackie Perry, Robert Peshka, Michael Pinkney, Dennis Ponczkowski, Patricia Price, Josef Puehringer, Gary & Cynthia Quinn (my brother and his wife), Maureen Rieckhof, Gail Robertson, the Rochester Agape Club, Patrick Salimi, Jan &

Bob Sanders (my mother and her husband). Richard and Carolyn Santee, Barbara Sarratori, Harvey G. Seybold, Joan Simmett, Norma & David Spall, Mary & Alan Temple, Toronto IPI #77, Steve Tucker, Janice Tuschong, Elaine Vanier, Roddy Vanier, Lew VonAlmen, Kimberly Walsh, Pastor William Yonker (Immanuel Lutheran Church), Elaine Webster, Chris & Gabrielle Weiss, Paula Wemp, Charlene Wood, Todd Zdanowski, and several people who wish to remain anonymous.

I wish to give a special acknowledgment to Peter Fromme-Douglas, for the amazing cover, wonderful photograph, and many illustrations. I will always remember the afternoon we came up with this outrageous title.

To my editor and webmaster, Brandi Jasmine, all I can say is how much gratitude I feel for how good you have made me look, and how patient you have been with me … this book will reach more people because of you.

Lloyd Steven Sieden, I cannot express to you how much I appreciate your Foreword to this book. The first time I read it, I felt as if Buckminster Fuller himself was introducing me through you. You are a gifted writer and I am humbled to have your support.

To my mother, Janet Eve Sanders, I need to say how profoundly you have affected my life. Your living example taught me of *Love-Based* leadership long before I learned the term. No 'thank you' can be enough, but thank you.

I must also honor my father, James H. Quinn. Your footprints can be found on almost every page of this book. You were my mentor, my business partner, and my friend … and I miss you.

Finally, I thank my students. You have come from many different backgrounds, cultures, and nationalities. You have taught me far more than I could possibly have taught you. Most importantly, I have learned that despite the uniqueness of varying peoples and cultures, inside we have more similarities than differences.

Thank You All,

Ross

> *"Never doubt that a small group of committed citizens can change the world.*
> *Indeed, it is the only thing that ever has."*
>
> … Margaret Mead

References

Alessandra, Tony & Cathcart, Jim, *Relationship Strategies*, Nightingale-Conant Corp.

Ansari, Mahfooz, *Managing People at Work: Leadership Styles and Influence Strategies*, Sage Publications, 1991

Arrien, Angeles, *The Four Fold Way*, Harper San Francisco, 1993

Atkins, Stuart, *The Name of Your Game: Four Game Plans for Success at Home & at Work*, Ellis & Stewart, 1982

Bamborough, J.B.; Dodsworth, Martin; Burton, Robert; *Anatomy of Melancholy (Vol 6)*, Clarendon Press, 2001

Baron, Renee, *What Type Am I: Discover Who You Really Are*, Penguin USA, 1998

Batra, Dr. Ravi, *The Great Depression of 1990*, Simon and Schuster, 1987

Benson, Herbert, *The Relaxation Response*, HarperCollins Publishers, 2000

Bolton, Robert & Dorothy, G., *Social Style/Management Style*, AMACOM, 1984

Brewer, J. H., Ainsworth, J. M., & Wynne, G. E., *Power Management*, Prentice-Hall, 1984

Bristol, Claude, *The Magic of Believing*, Pocket Books, 1994

Buscalia, Leo, *Love*, Ballantine Books, 1996

Covey, Stephen, *The 7 Habits of Highly Effective People*, Simon & Schuster, 1990

De Ville, Jard, *Nice Guys Finish First: How to Get People to Do What You Want, and Thank You For It.*, William Morrow, 1979

Dryden, Gordon & Vos, Jeannette, *The Learning Revolution*, Jalmar Press, 1994

Everett, Alexander, Inward Bound, *Living Life From The Inside Out*, Bookpartners Inc, 1998

Fuller, R. Buckminster, *Critical Path*, St. Martin's Press, 2002

Ganza, Ann, *Journey of Hope, Remembering Mother Teresa's Spirit*, Agnel Publishing, 2001

Gray, Dr John, *Men Are From Mars Women Are From Venus*, Harper Collins, 1993

Geier, John G., *(D.I.S.C.) Personal Profile System*, Performax Systems International, 1977

Hansen, Mark Victor, *The One Minute Millionaire*, Harmony Books, 2002

Hartman, Taylor, PhD, *The Color Code*, Scribner, 1987

Hawkins, David R., *Power vs. Force*, Hay House, 2002

Hermann, Ned, *The Creative Brain*, Brain Books, 1991

Hill, Napoleon, *Think and Grow Rich*, Fawcett Books, 1990

Hill, Richard, *The Best of Organization Development: From Training and Development Journa*l, American Society for Training & Development, 1988

Hill, Ruth Beebe, *Hanta Yo*, Doubleday & Company, 1979

Horrell, Edward, *More Than Words*, e-book

Hunsaker, Phillip L., *The Art of Managing People*, Prentice Hall, 1980

Jampolski, Jerry, *Love is Letting Go of Fear*, Celestial Arts, 1988

Jaynes, J., *The Origin of Consciousness in the Breakdown of the Bicameral Mind*, Houghton Mifflin, 1977

Jung, Carl Gustav, *Psychological Types (Collected Works of C.G. Jung Vol.6)*, Princeton University Press, 1976

Keirsey, David, *Please Understand Me. Character & Temperament Types*, Prometheus, 1984

Lefton, Robert E., *Effective Motivation Through Performance Appraisal: Dimensional Appraisal Strategies*, John Wiley & Sons, 1977

LeTellier, John, *Quantum Learning*, Dell Publishing, 1992

Lovas, Michael, *Face Values*

Maltz, Maxwell, *Psychocybernetics*, Pocket Books, 1989

Marston, William M., *Emotions of Normal People*, Personna Press, 1979

Maslow, Abraham H., *The Farther Reaches of Human Nature*, Viking Press, 1971

Merrill, David, & Reid, Roger, *Personal Styles & Effective Performance*, Saint Lucie, 1981

Miscisin, Mary, *Showing Our True Colors*, True Colors, Inc, 2001

Myers, Isabel Briggs. & Myers, Peter B., *Gifts Differing: Understanding Personality*, Consulting Psychologists Press, 1997

New International Version, Holy Bible, International Bible Society, 1984

Pease, Allan, *Questions are the Answers, Pease Training International Ltd.*, 2000

Rand, Ayn, *Atlas Shrugged*, Signet, 1996

Redfield, James, *The Celestine Prophecy*, Warner Books, 1993

Rowling, J. K., *Harry Potter and the Sorcerer's Stone*, Arthur A. Levine Books, 1997

Rosenban, David, & Seligman, Martin E.P., *Abnormal Psychology*, W.W. Norton & Co, 1989

Ruiz, Don Miguel, *The Four Agreements*, Amber-Publishing, 1997

Saltzman, David, *The Jester Has Lost His Jingle*, Jester Co. Inc., 1995

Sieden, Lloyd Steven, *Buckminster Fuller's Universe: His Life and Work*, Perseus, 2000

Sun Bear, *Medicine Wheel, Earth Astrology*, Fireside, 1980

Stearn, Jess, *The Power of Alpha Thinking*, New American Library, 1989

Teresa, Mother, *A Simple Path*, Ballantine Books, 1995

Wilson Learning Corporation, *Social Styles Sales Strategies*, 1977